HISTORIC
ARTS & CRAFTS
HOMES
of GREAT BRITAIN

HISTORIC
ARTS & CRAFTS
HOMES
of GREAT BRITAIN

Brian D. Coleman

Gibbs Smith, Publisher
Salt Lake City

This book is dedicated to my dear friend Peter Rose,
travel companion and tour guide extraordinaire.

First Edition
09 08 07 06 05   5 4 3 2 1

Published by
Gibbs Smith, Publisher
P.O. Box 667
Layton, Utah 84041

Orders: 1.800.748.5439
www.gibbs-smith.com

Designed by Linda Herman
Printed and bound in Hong Kong

Library of Congress Cataloging-in-Publication Data

Coleman, Brian D.
  Historic arts & crafts homes of Great Britain / Brian D. Coleman.—1st ed.
    p. cm.

  ISBN 1-58685-531-X
  1. Architecture, Domestic—Great Britain. 2. Arts and crafts
movement—Great Britain. 3. Interior decoration—Great Britain. I. Title:
Historic arts and crafts homes of Great Britain. II. Title.

NA7328.C624 2005
728'.0941—dc22

2005010960

CONTENTS

THE ARTS AND CRAFTS HOUSE IN BRITAIN

by Stephen Calloway

The great protagonists of the Arts and Crafts cause were in a real sense revolutionaries. The artists, craftsmen, thinkers and writers, architects and designers who initiated the movement in the second half of the nineteenth century and those who carried it forward into the twentieth shared an ideal of changing the world no less passionate, and a vision of the future every bit as optimistic, as those of the political revolutionaries of 1789, of 1848 or of 1917.

That this revolution was to be an entirely peaceful one does not mean that its aim was any less radical. But this would be an uprising of makers, not destroyers; of artists and aesthetes, not iconoclasts. These high-minded revolutionaries had no wish to pull down governments or depose kings. They sought, however, nothing less than the overthrow of what they perceived to be an iniquitous social order, a system founded upon the exploitation and degradation of labour; a system based upon greed that filled the marketplace with shoddy goods and a commercial world that found the inevitable expression of its debased values in the ever-increasing ugliness of modern life.

The desire of these revolutionaries was to bring about a new artistic and social order not by forcing change and innovation upon an unwilling public but, rather, by showing that there was a better way to live. This improvement would be achieved, they believed, in large part, by a return to the old ways. Their goal was to re-create a world in which beauty could again triumph over meanness, ugliness and utilitarian compromise. By championing the old craft skills against the power of the machine, they aimed at the reversal of the inexorable and overwhelming trend of nineteenth-century "progress" towards the production of almost all everyday goods in soulless factory conditions. The men and women of the Arts and Crafts movement sought, above all, to transform manufacture and thereby to change society, bringing content and delight to the rich man and the poor alike through the making of beautiful things. In the joys of fine craftsmanship lay the answer to the besetting miseries

"The Wykhamist" by C. F. A. Voysey.
Courtesy of Trustworth Studio.

of the age; all would achieve happiness, either as the reward of honest work or through living well in the possession of Beauty.

The quintessential expression of these lofty but, as they fervently believed, universally applicable ideas lay in the creation of the "House Beautiful." Not surprisingly, this was an ideal most readily achievable by the rich, but it remained a concept that, at its most utopian, aimed at the improvement of not only the mansion of the wealthy patron but also the simple dwelling of the working man.

The idea of a house fashioned, for those who could afford it, from top to bottom according to the vision and design of a single artist or architect was, of course, nothing new; in the early eighteenth century William Kent had been celebrated for the care that he bestowed upon devising the entire look of his projects, specifying everything from the plan of the house and its every architectural flourish down to the shape of a chair or table, the fall of a drapery and the moulding of a picture frame. Adam, Wyatt, Soane and many other architects of the late eighteenth and early nineteenth centuries had revealed a similar genius for dictating the interior decoration, choosing colours and fabrics and designing the furniture for their houses. But such architects held themselves aloof from their craftsmen and tradesmen, expecting them to follow design drawings and the written specifications of works to the letter. Even Pugin, the first passionate advocate of a return not just to the styles but also to the architectural and decorative principles of the medieval period, had been obliged to work wholly within the established commercial system of builders, decorators and upholsterers to realise his idiosyncratic gothic vision.

William Morris, the founding father of the Arts and Crafts and the tireless powerhouse of the early days of the movement, was the first to approach the whole question of design and manufacture in a new way. Beginning essentially as an amateur (he had originally been destined as a student at Oxford to enter the church), Morris gained only a little architectural training in the office of the respected gothic revivalist G. E. Street before deciding upon a life devoted to art and poetry. Having fallen under the influence of the Pre-Raphaelite poet-painter Dante Gabriel Rossetti, and already in love with the literature and legend of the Middle Ages, Morris made the great intellectual leap of seeing in the art, the buildings and the craftsmanship of that distant era a viable model for reforming the ills of modern industrial society.

To Morris and to other thinkers, such as John Ruskin, the impoverishment of the visual and material culture of the day appeared as a damning indictment of both the gross social inequalities and the creeping banality and imaginative impoverishment of the modern world. The great answer, as Morris would argue over a period of forty years of ceaseless activity, lay in reversing the century's headlong rush towards urbanisation, capitalist trade, factory production and the division of labour, in favour of a return to ancient traditions of both work and social organisation. The reform and salvation of the nineteenth century was, he

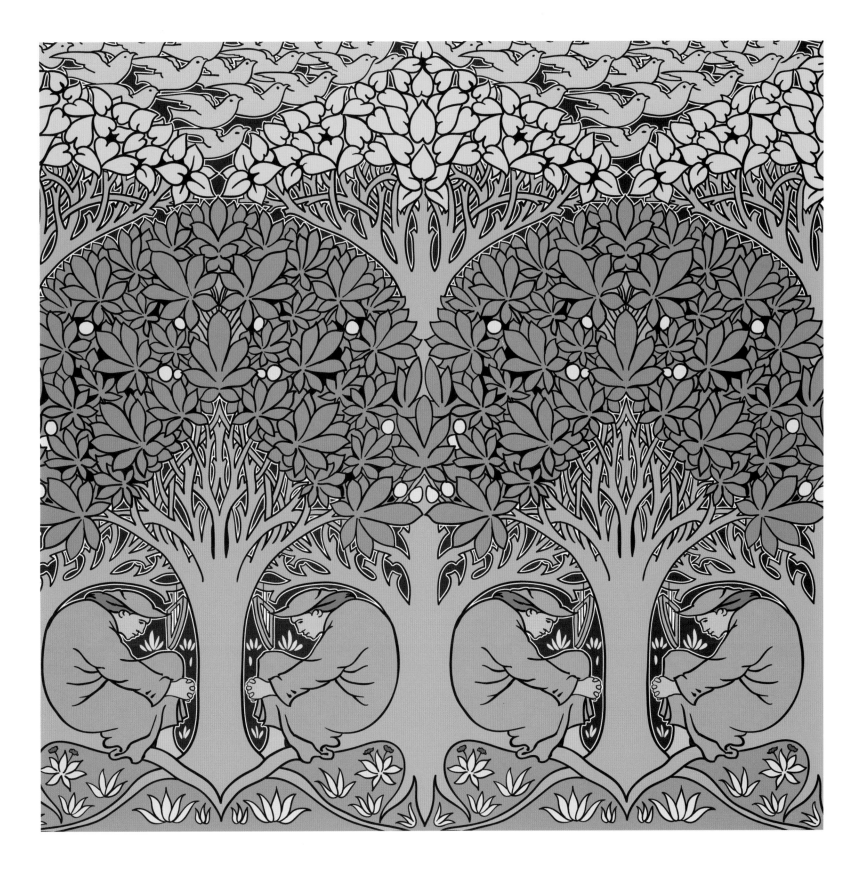

suggested, to be achieved only by a return to the wholesome ideals of an earlier age. Morris urged in particular the adoption of the ethos of the medieval guildsmen and master craftsmen. These were men, Morris believed, who had pride in their skills and knew the value of fine materials. They were, crucially, designer-makers who understood every process of their trade and took delight in the making of beautiful objects, simple in structure and adorned with meaningful ornament. Working in this way, Morris hoped, workmen would once again be their own masters, employed by enlightened and honourable patrons; how could such men fail to take pride in their work and live fulfilling lives?

When, in 1861, Morris and his Pre-Raphaelite friends Dante Gabriel Rossetti and Edward Burne-Jones formed "The Firm," a loose association of "Art-Workmen," it was a revolutionary step. Their first, almost achingly earnest productions: heavy chairs, tables and cabinets designed by Morris himself, by Ford Madox Brown and by the architect Philip Webb and painted by Rossetti and Burne-Jones, were based on the gawky, medievalising pieces that the circle had originally made for their own use and amusement; they must have seemed extraordinarily crude to eyes accustomed to the slick furnishings of the London trade. These first pieces created something of a stir at the big International Exhibition staged in London in 1862.

It is, however, to Red House at Bexley, the home that Philip Webb designed for the newly married Morris and to which their whole circle contributed decorative elements, that we must look to see the first full realisation of Morris's vision of the House Beautiful. Red House was conceived as a complete work of art, as a statement of intent and also as the home of an idealist and a poet. It is a vision at once highly romantic and curiously down-to-earth. Here Morris and his friends let their imaginations soar towards the realisation of a fairy-tale version of the medieval interior; yet here, too, we can observe them as practical men taking their first, sometimes tentative, steps towards the mastery of many trades.

Driven by Morris's passion to master all the ancient processes, including dying and tapestry weaving, manuscript illumination and calligraphy or the intricacies of block-cutting and printing, the productions of The Firm, without ever losing their essential strength and integrity of design and materials, became increasingly sophisticated. From its beginnings with medievalising furniture, painted and embroidered panels and tiles, The Firm's activities came to embrace hand-printed wallpapers, printed and woven fabrics, tapestry, carpets, metalwork, stained glass, ceramics and, in the last decade of the century, the exquisite books that Morris printed at his Kelmscott Press.

None in Morris's immediate circle of friends and associates, nor indeed any single figure in the great wave of followers that formed the wider Arts and Crafts movement, could claim to have made so many crafts their own. Nor could any rival the rich and seemingly never-ending stream of writings that he appeared to pour forth so effortlessly; this great body of work would run, eventually, to many thousands of pages and include long prose romances,

OPPOSITE: *"Dove and Holly" by C. F. A. Voysey. Courtesy of Trustworth Studio.*

epic and lyric verse, translations, practical manuals and lectures and many spirited socialist polemics. When Morris died in 1896, aged only sixty-two, it was said that the great war horse and warrior bard had exhausted himself by doing in a single lifetime the work of ten lesser men.

Red House remains still, it might be argued, the single most important and iconic building of the Arts and Crafts. After Morris sold the place and moved back to London and then to Kelmscott Manor in Oxfordshire, Red House belonged for a time to another great protagonist of the movement, Charles Holme, proprietor and editor of *The Studio* magazine. But after him, the house fell upon hard times. Fortunately, at a point in the 1950s when its future looked very bleak, it was saved by the architect Edward Hollamby, who for many years cared for the structure and made heroic attempts to restore and care for the interiors. Red House is now happily secure in the ownership of the National Trust, its rooms returned as closely as is presently possible to their original appearance. In many ways, the other houses revealed in this book—widespread as they are and widely varying in their styles and scale of simplicity or grandeur—all owe their existence to Morris's pioneering inspiration. Each in its way bears the imprint of Morris's own practise or, more abstractly, of his thinking. In some—at Standen and Wightwick perhaps most clearly—we see a direct continuation of the decorative styles and eclectic aesthetic principles that Morris initiated. In others—especially at Blackwell, Cragside or the extraordinary Castle Drogo—we can savour the spirit of Morris's ideas of the House Beautiful expressed in a new, confident and often startling architectural language. And, finally, who could doubt that for all its quirky Bloomsbury modernism, Charleston is also a quintessential expression of Englishness in the Arts and Crafts tradition.

Throughout all the wonderful rooms featured in these pages resonates a single shining phrase penned by William Morris; it is a celebrated thought from one of his lectures, a line destined to become the great mantra of the Arts and Crafts movement: "Have nothing in your houses which you do not know to be useful or believe to be beautiful."

Introduction

As a dyed-in-the-wool Victorian aesthete, five years ago I never would have thought I would be writing a book on historic Arts and Crafts homes in Great Britain. But as I began writing more articles on the movement in my role as editor-at-large for *Old House Interiors* magazine I became increasingly fascinated with William Morris and his influence in both our country and England. Soon I began finding excuses to visit the U.K. and see where it all began—I traveled from the scenic lochs of Scotland to the pastoral hills of the Cotswolds, touring every historic Arts and Crafts home I could find. And thus the idea for this book was born.

While there are hundreds of historic homes in Great Britain, truly Arts and Crafts examples are limited to a handful. I chose my ten favorite, making sure that each was open and accessible to the public. I tried to include not only the most famous, such as William Morris's Red House and Kelmscott Manor, but a few of the more eccentric ones as well—Lutyen's feudal Castle Drogo and my favorite, the free-wheeling and impressionistic Charleston. Many involved quite a journey—Mackintosh's still-modern Hill House, located in the scenic countryside outside of Glasgow was a several day trip from London. But each was a memorable and fascinating experience and provided me with invaluable insight into the creativity and genius of the architects and designers of the Arts and Crafts period.

John Ruskin had first written about the importance of truth in architecture and the attainment of personal satisfaction through individual craftsmanship in his book *The Stones of Venice* (1853), and many architects and designers of the period were fascinated with his work, including a young William Morris struggling to find himself after his university years at Oxford. Following a brief period apprenticing in architect Edmund Street's office in 1856, Morris realized he was best suited to working on his own as an artist and designer. Blessed with a family inheritance that made it unnecessary for him to earn an outside income, Morris was able to follow his own muse; thus, he formed his now-famous design company, Morris & Co. with fellow artists and architects, including Edward Burne-Jones, Philip Webb and Dante Gabriel Rossetti.

Morris started in 1860 by building his own home, the Red House, in a rural suburb of London; it was not long before commissions for his unique textiles and wallpapers multiplied.

OPPOSITE: *"Elsa" by J.R. Burrows and Company.*

But the Red House was the only home Morris was to ever own outright. After only five years, he returned to London to be closer to his business, and then took out a long-term lease on Kelmscott Manor, a sixteenth-century farmhouse deep in the Cotswolds. Morris grew to love his time spent in the fresh, country air and surrounding meadows at Kelmscott, and many of his most popular designs were inspired by the gardens and wildlife he sketched during his stays. Kelmscott was fortunately preserved by his widow and daughters and is now run by the Society of Antiquaries of London, which has restored it with many original furnishings, supplemented by some from Morris's London home as well.

Other architects actively working and designing during this period were close friends of Morris who shared his ideals and vision. One of these was Philip Webb, who had first met Morris while both were working in Edmund Street's architectural offices in London. While Morris did not last long as an architect, Webb continued in the profession and built a select but respectable practice. Morris was one of his first and best clients, and engaged Webb to design and help furnish the Red House. Webb would go on to design similar homes for others, but was always insistent that the homeowners share his ideals of artistic yet practical homes. One such residence is Standen, designed between 1892 and 1894 for London solicitor James Beale, his wife, Margaret, and their large family of seven children. Nestled into a slope on the site of a medieval Sussex farm, Standen is an outstanding example of the combination of vernacular materials with the exquisite detailing and hand craftsmanship of the Arts and Crafts period. The interiors and grounds have now been handsomely restored and the house is an inspiration to any Arts and Crafts enthusiast.

As Morris's influence grew, his firm's products became more and more popular. One rare surviving example of how they were installed in the late nineteenth century has been preserved at Wightwick Manor in central England. Built between 1887 and 1888 with a substantial addition in 1893, Wightwick was designed by architect Edward Ould for the wealthy Wolverhampton paint manufacturer Theodore Mander. The Liverpool architect specialized in the construction of Old English–style homes, purposefully designed to look as if they had been built centuries earlier, with exposed half timbering, irregular massing and multiple gables topped by large, ornate chimney stacks. Quaint details, such as inspirational quotes carved on the windows and above the doors, and small, irregularly placed windows added to the charm. Theodore Mander was an ardent supporter of the Arts and Crafts ideals and was able to furnish his home with the latest and most beautiful products available. Most of the rooms were papered with William Morris patterns, and Morris & Co.'s textiles were used for drapery and upholstery. Eamer Kempe, a well-known stained-glass artist of the period, was engaged to design glowing stained-glass panels for the windows on themes as broad as the Arthurian legends and the Virtues (including Temperance, as Mander was a teetotaler). Later generations of the family continued to add to the Arts and Crafts interiors, and

OPPOSITE: *"Coleman Bower" by J.R. Burrows and Company.*

Wightwick Manor now boasts an outstanding collection of Pre-Raphaelite art as well. Given to the National Trust in 1937, Wightwick remains a much-loved family home as well as a testimonial to the beauty of Morris & Co.'s products.

Cragside, the country retreat of English inventor and businessman Lord William Armstrong, was designed by Richard Norman Shaw between 1870 and 1884. Originally a simple hunting lodge in the Northumberland hills of northeastern England, Cragside became a rambling country manor built in the picturesque Old English style, based on medieval manors and barns of southern England. As Armstrong was a scientist, the home boasted all of the latest amenities, including the first hydraulic-powered electricity in the world, central heating, telephones, even a Turkish bath. Armstrong furnished his home with work of the best Arts and Crafts designers, including luminous stained-glass windows from Morris & Co and a breathtaking two-story carved-Italian marble inglenook and fireplace designed by W. R. Lethaby, Shaw's chief assistant. Surrounded by a thousand acres of landscaped gardens, woodlands, streams and lakes, all added by Armstrong to the originally barren, rocky slopes, Cragside remains a tribute to the ingenuity and fortitude of Lord Armstrong.

Of course, not all Arts and Crafts homes were furnished solely by Morris & Co. Many, in fact, used local craftsmen, following the Arts and Crafts emphasis on vernacular design. Rodmarton Manor, built in the scenic Cotswolds over a twenty-year period between 1909 and 1929, was designed by local Cotswolds architect Earnest Barnsley for Claud Biddulph, a wealthy stockbroker. The Biddulphs wanted a large country home whose construction would provide a source of employment for the local craftspeople, reviving their talents and, so, serving the community. All of the furniture was designed and built locally, but a few outside experts were recruited to help, such as Alfred and Louise Powell, well-known artists for Wedgwood Pottery who were asked to paint furniture and design ceramics for the house. Kept intact by succeeding generations, Rodmarton Manor is still owned and occupied by the Biddulphs.

Large country homes were an important tradition in England until World War I, and one of their most prolific architects was Sir Edward Lutyens. Lutyens' trademark was vernacular Arts and Crafts buildings based upon Georgian and Classical styles. But Lutyens also designed other celebrated homes, such as Castle Drogo in southwestern Devon for wealthy businessman Julius Drewe. Built between 1909 and 1929, Castle Drogo was Drewe's ancestral confabulation, a modern-day castle that his ancestors could have built when they first came to England with William the Conqueror. Constructed of local granite on a steep promontory overlooking a river valley below, Castle Drogo combined romantic touches—such as slit windows, turrets and buttresses, even a portcullis over the front door—with modern conveniences such as the latest rib cage shower fittings. Tapestries and Georgian furniture were used to furnish the severe and stark interiors. While the family continues to live in part of the castle today, this National Trust property has been open for tours since 1974.

OPPOSITE: *"Priory Garden" by J.R. Burrows and Company.*

Castles were, in fact, popular throughout the United Kingdom. Hill House, built in 1902 outside of Glasgow by the famous Scottish architect Charles Rennie Mackintosh, was designed for publisher Walter W. Blackie, who wanted something other than quaint plaster-and-beamed walls, brick facades and red-tile roofs. Mackintosh understood Blackie's wishes perfectly and designed a Scottish baronial castle but styled it in the avant-garde taste of the early twentieth century: modern in design and honest, with the massing of its parts forming the architecture. Mackintosh designed every detail of the interiors—from the geometric, angular rooms with abstract friezes of stylized roses, to the striking, ebonized furniture that, in reality, was not at all comfortable. Color was strictly dictated by Mackintosh in each room, a palette of blacks and whites, offset by soft grays, pinks and blues.

Blackwell, in the scenic Lake District of northwestern England, is another large country home built in the Arts and Crafts tradition. Designed by H. M. Baillie Scott for wealthy Manchester brewery owner Sir Chester Holt, his wife and their family of five children, it was built between 1898 and 1900 as a family country retreat. Baillie Scott, whose work is reminiscent of C. F. A. Voysey, emphasized the importance of living in harmony with nature and integrated references to nature throughout the house, from rowan berries of the local native ash to motifs including bluebells, Lakeland daisies, bluebirds and roses, all used repeatedly in carvings, stained glass and plasterwork throughout the home. The Holts only used their summer home infrequently and it was never modernized or changed. Rescued from an uncertain fate in 1999, Blackwell was opened in 2001 as a house museum.

The Arts and Crafts tradition of local craftsmanship and design was carried into the twentieth century by an iconoclastic group of artists who called themselves The Bloomsbury Group. Named after the home in which they first held gatherings in London, in 1916 several of its members moved to the Sussex countryside and leased an ancient stone farmhouse, Charleston, where they would continue to live and create for the next sixty years. Described as "odd and preposterous people" by their peers, they were free thinkers and anti-establishment; the group included a number of famous authors and artists, including Virginia Woolf and Roger Fry. They began decorating the house immediately, filling it with junk-market finds that they hand painted in bold Post-Impressionistic colors and patterns. Wallpaper was painted out with striking freehand drawings, doors and even fireplaces were covered with stencils and pictures, and handmade light fixtures and curtains were added. Described as "absurdly overdecorated" by conventional friends, Charleston was an ode to the creativity and craftsmanship of its occupants.

Historic homes are some of England's greatest treasures, and those that celebrate the Arts and Crafts movement form an integral part. I hope this book will broaden the reader's insight and understanding into the origins of the Arts and Crafts movement's philosophy and design, and that everyone enjoys these inspiring homes as much as I did.

OPPOSITE: *"Bird and Bramble" by C. F. A. Voysey. Courtesy Trustworth Studio.*

BLACKWELL HOUSE

Blackwell is the only surviving work by the Arts and Crafts architect M. H. Baillie Scott that is open to the public. Considered one of his finest and largest commissions, Blackwell was built between 1898 and 1890 as the holiday home of wealthy Manchester brewery owner Sir Edward Holt, his wife, Elizabeth, and their five children. Sited in the scenic Lake District of northwestern England on a hill above the blue waters of Windermere, Blackwell was intended as an escape from the pollution and congestion that characterized industrial Manchester in the late 1800s. Blackwell escaped the fate of modernization and remodeling; even its interior decorations were kept remarkably intact. Blackwell was rescued from an uncertain fate in 1999 by the Lakeland Arts Trust, and after undergoing a £3,500,000 ($7,000,000) restoration, was opened to the public in 2001 as one of England's most beautiful Arts and Crafts house museums.

Sir Edward Holt was active in local government and charities, improving libraries, building waterworks and aiding local charities. He helped develop a reservoir in the Lake District that revolutionized the supply of freshwater to Manchester. It seemed sensible, then, for him to build a house where he could monitor the reservoir's progress. As he looked for an architect, it was not surprising that he called upon Baillie Scott, for by the 1890s, Baillie Scott was becoming a well-known name in the Arts and Crafts community. A regular contributor to magazines such as The Studio, his work was reminiscent of contemporary Arts and Crafts architects such as C. F. A. Voysey and Charles Rennie Mackintosh. In 1897 Baillie Scott had won a commission for the decorations and furnishings for the Grand Duke of Hesse's palace at Darmstadt, Germany, and received much international acclaim for his work; it was shortly after this that Sir Holt asked him to design Blackwell. As this was not the Holt's primary residence, the practical requirements for day-to-day living, accommodating children, etc., were not as important, Baillie Scott was given free reign to design the home based on his philosophy of architecture, which was rooted in an Arts and Crafts aesthetic, and emphasized the

TOP: *The terraces afford sweeping vistas and fells of Windermere.* BOTTOM: *During the 1940s, Blackwell became a school. Here, girls are skating on the terrace.*

importance of living in harmony with nature, and valued light, texture and space in the interiors.

Sir Holt also hired the Simpsons of Kendal to produce the interior paneling and carvings. Arthur Simpson and his son Hubert's business, called The Handicrafts, produced beautifully made Arts and Crafts furniture and carvings from 1895 until 1952.

Unfortunately, there is scant information on the construction of Blackwell and on the Holt family while they lived there. While Scott designed striking Arts and Crafts interiors based on themes of nature, it is known that the Holts actually furnished Blackwell with Edwardian and Victorian pieces they already owned. Nonetheless, Baillie Scott's carved ornament and mantels, stained-glass windows and fitted furniture still remain.

Blackwell was to be one of Baillie Scott's largest commissions; in later years he was best known for his designs of smaller cottages for "people with artistic aspirations but modest incomes." Blackwell became a school in 1941 and remained so until 1976; then it was briefly used as a health club and finally was leased as offices until it was restored as a public house museum and tribute to Baillie Scott's masterful Arts and Crafts design.

The setting of the house was important in Baillie Scott's plans, as it was meant to be a place of relaxation—a retreat where the Holts could appreciate the beauty of nature and lift their spirits. Themes from nature were used throughout the house—rowan berries of the local mountain ash were the principal motif in the downstairs rooms, and other naturalistic designs such as bluebirds and berries, Lakeland daisies, bluebells and roses were incorporated in everything from stained glass to plasterwork and wood carvings. The exterior of the

The north facade of Blackwell shows the striking white roughcast exterior. Note the touches such as the cylindrical chimney pots, which are typical of the region.

house makes an impressive statement, but one that is interpreted in a vernacular way. Baillie Scott used the local Lakeland farmhouses of the sixteenth and seventeenth centuries as his inspiration, incorporating roughcast, whitewashed walls, steeply pitched slate roofs, cylindrical chimneys and sandstone mullions, but updated the style by keeping decoration to a minimum and setting windows flush with the facade for a crisp and sharp profile.

The house is sited high on the hillside with commanding views of the lake and fells. The main rooms on the reception floor face south, rather than west across the lake, to take advantage of the sunlight. Color was carefully considered, and the warm tones of honey-colored oak paneling were contrasted against white walls that shimmered with light. Green slate and pink sandstone, copper lighting and multicolored marbles were all used to heighten the effect. Corridors upstairs and downstairs give a prelude of the rooms beyond with paneling and carvings, and the level of light is cleverly adjusted by increasing the size of the windows as one passes farther down the corridor.

Baillie Scott wanted to break away from typical Victorian floor plans with small, cluttered rooms, so they designed a main hall as the home's focal point, around which other rooms

OPPOSITE: *Considered one of Baillie Scott's most spectacular rooms, the White Parlor is centered on a graceful fireplace adorned with slender columns and an inglenook. Even the ceiling has plaster ornament of flowers and birds.* TOP: *The white paneling in the corridor anticipates entrance to the White Parlor.* BELOW: *Gracefully carved capitals of leaves, fruits and birds adorn the top of the fireplace columns.*

were arranged. The principal room for entertaining, the main hall evokes the feeling of a medieval castle with its two-story, half-timbered ceiling; tall, stained-glass windows with Sir Edward Holt's coat of arms; and large fireplace with inglenooks on each side. Local craftsmen were used in accordance with Baillie Scott's Arts and Crafts philosophy, influenced, no doubt, by John Ruskin's famous statement "Good art flows from the craftsmen who create it." Thus, the oak-paneled lower walls of the main hall were embellished with a frieze of intertwined rowan berries carved by the Simpsons of Kendal. An original wallpaper frieze of prancing peacocks at the top of the walls is miraculously still intact. The family had a billiards table in the center of the hall, and while the table is no longer present, the original dish-shaped copper lights were found during restoration and reinstalled. A Manxman piano was purchased by the Lakeland Trust to sit at one end of the hall. Designed by Baillie Scott for a different house to look like a piece of furniture, the piano was disguised as an elegant cupboard, its keys hidden behind doors with large strap hinges extending around the sides, ending in a fleur-de-lys pattern. Baillie Scott included a whimsical minstrels' gallery above the fireplace, creating a cozy inglenook underneath.

Opening off the main hall, the dining room continues the baronial feeling with its oak-paneled walls and ceiling. Carved rowan berries are continued as a frieze below the ceiling. A large fireplace with walk-in inglenooks creates a sense of warmth and welcome. Baillie Scott designed a block-printed Hessian frieze of stylized bluebells, daisies and bluebirds that is still intact on the walls. Blue was felt to be an appropriate color for the dining room due

ABOVE: *The carved-oak paneling continues in the upstairs hall, where light is provided by skylights and windows.* RIGHT: *Oak-paneled walls and ceiling continue in the dining room. The wall covering was designed by Baillie Scott in a stylized motif of the elements of nature—birds, daisies and bluebells.* OPPOSITE: *This bedroom, painted in sunny yellow, adopted its color scheme from a fireplace lined with William De Morgan tiles, as did each bedroom in the home.*

to its calming qualities, and sunlight in the dining area was considered vulgar, so Baillie Scott designed the room with shades of blue in the wall coverings, and windows were kept small, decorated with stylized stained-glass tulips and birds.

The white drawing room on the opposite side of the main hall is considered to be one of Baillie Scott's finest interiors. In contrast to the dark, masculine main hall, the drawing room is bright and delicate, filled with sunlight. Intricate carvings of birds, berries and flowers are highlighted in the ceiling plasterwork. The white paneling on the walls even has small inset mirrors in it to further capture the sunlight throughout the day. The focal point of the room is the fireplace and inglenook, accented by slender, tapering columns capped by carved wooden capitals of leaves and fruits. Swaying tulips and birds adorn the stained-glass windows, and even the tall iron firedogs continue the theme of nature with enameled red berries and white flowers.

The remainder of the house—the servants' quarters and kitchen downstairs, and the bedrooms upstairs—have been restored for modern use but follow Baillie Scott's principles, with clean, simple lines and careful detailing and workmanship. All of the bedrooms originally had fireplaces lined with William De Morgan tiles, and the colors of the rooms were taken from the tiles.

Blackwell is located at Bowness on Windermere in the picturesque Lakes District. Call or visit the website for opening times and directions: 01144 15394 46139; www.blackwell.org.uk ❧

CASTLE DROGO

Sir Edward Lutyens (1869–1944) was a prolific architect of the late nineteenth and first half of the twentieth centuries, designing more than three hundred country homes and buildings, from the Viceroy's House in New Delhi (1912) to the Midland Bank in London (1928). But he was known particularly for his country homes based on vernacular Georgian and Classical styles. The same age as Frank Lloyd Wright, one year younger than Charles Rennie Mackintosh and twelve years younger than C. F. A. Voysey, Lutyens was a contemporary of many of the well-known architects of his time. A testimonial to Lutyens' innate sense of design, he was able to build a solid and popular architectural practice with little formal education.

Lutyens spent his first years studying local seventeenth- and eighteenth-century farm buildings around his home in Surrey with Gertrude Jekyll, and learned to value simple materials and construction. After working for architect Sir Ernest George from 1887 to 1889, Lutyens opened his own office. Clients were typically wealthy industrialists or businessmen who had seen one of his homes in *Country Life*, which published his work regularly, and wanted a large home for entertaining their weekend guests in the country. Julius Drewe was just such a client. The founder of several very successful stores that imported goods from China and the colonies, Drewe rapidly made a large fortune and was able to retire at the age of thirty-three. While living in Sussex, he researched his genealogy and found that his family had descended from Drogo, or Dru, a noble Norman who had accompanied William the Conqueror to England. Drogo's descendants were established in Drewsteignton in southwestern England, and Drewe decided to erect his own castle there on his ancestor's home ground. He found a steep granite promontory to build upon that afforded sweeping views of the River Teign Valley below, and contacted Lutyens to help him design his castle. Lutyens had already designed two other homes from castle ruins, and thus he understood exactly what Drewe wanted.

ABOVE: *A wooden gate in the garden marks an allée of trees.* OPPOSITE: *Castle Drogo's battlements and turrets are glimpsed through a field of early spring daffodils.*

BELOW: *Front door latch.* RIGHT: *The south front of Castle Drogo presents an imposing first impression of a medieval fortress.* OPPOSITE: *A portcullis, which is lowered over the front door, protects the entrance tower.*

Initially plans called for a grand four-story castle with a two-story great hall, a barrel-vaulted drawing room, and even a three-story chapel. Drewe insisted on granite walls for authenticity, and as the cost mounted, successive plans were much reduced. Smaller living rooms and a modest chapel were finally agreed upon and work begun as granite was dug from a local quarry and brought to the construction site by traction engine and steam lorry. World War I broke out and halted construction; additionally, Drewe's eldest son was killed in 1917. In 1919 Drewe and his two surviving sons were determined to continue on with their castle but with a smaller staff and at a slower pace. In fact, it took another eleven years for work to be completed following Lutyens' plans, and the Drewes only finally moved into the house in 1927 as it was nearing completion.

A long, winding drive to the house and gardens edged by borders of clipped yews that complemented the castle outlines were installed as finishing touches. Julius Drewe died in 1931 and his second son, Basil, inherited Castle Drogo and maintained it as a family home. During World War II, Mrs. Julius Drewe and her daughter Mary ran the castle as a refuge for homeless children caught in the London bombings. Basil's son Anthony inherited the house in 1974 upon his father's death, and the family then decided to give the castle to the National Trust; they continue to live in apartments on the upper floors.

OPPOSITE: *Granite walls and arches in the entrance hall lead down the passageway to the dining room.*
ABOVE: *The dining room features mahogany paneling and an elaborate plasterwork ceiling.*

The arched entrance to Castle Drogo is guarded by a lion carved in stone above with the family motto in Latin underneath; there is even a portcullis that can be lowered to protect the castle from invaders. The hall is marked by bare granite walls and unpainted timbers, both treatments that are carried throughout the rest of the house. Massive granite arches support the cross walls of passages leading to other parts of the building. Furnishings include a Gobelins tapestry woven in the late seventeenth century, an early-seventeenth-century Spanish chest and other furniture brought from Drewe's previous home, Wadhurst Hall, in Sussex. Leading off the hall, the library is L-shaped, with the two sections being joined by a large granite arch. Billiards was played in the shorter leg of the room, while the longer section was used as a library and sitting room. Sixteenth-century Brussels tapestries and oak bookcases designed by Lutyens cover the walls, and the ceiling is constructed of coffered oak

panels for an intimate, masculine look. Lutyens paid attention to every detail, such as oak screens designed to hide the radiators.

From the library, large windows in the wide corridor give beautiful views of the surrounding landscape. A short flight of stairs leads to the drawing room. The paneling in the room is painted in a soft green, one of Lutyens' favorite techniques to offset the austerity of the rest of the house. Three walls of windows flood the room with light and give a beautiful view of the sloping hillside and river below. Furnishings are mostly from Drewe's previous home and include Chinese Chippendale chairs and a pair of George II gilt-wood mirrors. A portrait of Mrs. Julius Drewe hangs over the mantel.

The main stairs are the most striking feature of the house. Their scale is emphasized by the staircase ceiling, which begins at thirteen feet and is kept level the entire length of the stairs so that at the bottom the ceiling rises twenty-seven feet above the dining room door. Bare granite walls and archways, and a monumental forty-eight-light window make the space seem like a cathedral. Portraits of Julius and Mrs. Drewe decorate the landings.

OPPOSITE: *Mr. Drewe's dressing room has beautiful views over the Teign Gorge and is the first in a suite of three rooms. The round "rent audit" table, which revolves on its square base, is c. 1800; a pair of saddlebag armchairs is of the same period.* LEFT: *Mrs. Drewe's bedroom features a bay window overlooking the yew hedges. She used the desk in the window for her correspondence.* ABOVE, TOP: *Mrs. Drewe's bedroom with paneled walls and a stone fireplace.* ABOVE, LOWER: *The bathroom is set in a small tower; note the elaborate original shower on the left.*

ABOVE: *The chapel was the last part of the castle to be completed and was built between preexisting stone buttresses.* OPPOSITE: *The scullery is supported by massive granite pillars and lit by overhead lunette windows. All of the furnishings, from the teak drain boards to the chopping block, were designed by Lutyens.*

The dining room was a compromise—originally intended to be two stories, it was reduced to one story with the 1912 reduction in the size of the house plans. Lutyens made the room more intimate with a heavy coffered ceiling and mahogany paneling. Portraits of Julius Drewe and his family hang in the room.

The kitchen lies at the north end of the house and is partially underground as the hill slopes at this point. Built without windows, the kitchen is lit by a circular lantern in the ceiling, which provides natural light. Beneath it, a round table by Lutyens was used for food preparation. A scullery and larder were also designed for washing pots and pans and storing food supplies, and Lutyens designed most of the fittings.

The chapel originally was designed in the northwest corner of the castle where the drawing room was originally placed in 1912, before plans were abridged. Two buttresses, which had already been built, were used to form the walls of the chapel, and granite pillars were added to support the vaulted roof. Lit only by slit windows cut in the thick granite, the room is like a mystical secret chamber.

Castle Drogo is located in southwest England in Devon. It is a National Trust property. Visit their Web site for opening times and directions: www.nationaltrust.org.uk. Telephone: 011 44 1647 433306.

CHARLESTON

The Bloomsbury Group, a collection of writers, authors and intellectuals who began meeting at the turn of the twentieth century in a house in Bloomsbury, London, was for many years considered a collection of "odd and preposterous people" by their peers. Free thinkers and anti-establishment, they included a number of famous authors and artists such as T. S. Eliot and Roger Frye.

In 1916 two of the group's founders, painters Vanessa Bell and Duncan Grant, discovered a modest sixteenth-century farmhouse with an overgrown garden in the countryside of East Sussex and decided to move there, along with Vanessa's two children and Duncan's friend David Garnett. They began decorating the house immediately and continued for the next sixty years, filling it with junk-market finds, which they hand-painted in bold, postimpressionistic colors and patterns. Wallpaper was painted over with striking freehand designs; doors and even fireplaces were covered with stencils and pictures; and handmade light fixtures and curtains were added. Described as "absurdly overdecorated" by conventional friends, the house, called Charleston, soon became a favorite artistic haven for the avant-garde. Despite its discomforts—there was no hot water or central heat for many years—intellectuals and artists, from Maynard Keynes (he wrote his famous *Economic Consequences of Peace* in an upstairs bedroom at Charleston) to Virginia Woolf (Vanessa's sister), T. S. Eliot and E. M. Forster—all were frequent guests. Free-wheeling art, conversation and relationships flourished—Vanessa Bell's daughter, Angelica, by Duncan Grant eventually married Grant's own lover, David Garnett Yupin in 1942. Vanessa died at Charleston in 1961 at the age of eighty-one, while Duncan Grant lived until 1978, when he died at the age of ninety-three.

By then the house was in terrible repair, saturated with damp and mildew and overrun with pests. The fragile painting and artwork, much of it never intended to be permanent, was falling to pieces. During their lifetimes the artists had not worried about upkeep or maintenance since the house was leased, so if something wore out they simply painted over

OPPOSITE: *The unpretentious front door to the old farmhouse was painted a soft blue-grey.* ABOVE: *A walled garden was created behind the house, planted with seasonal vegetables, fruit and colorful annuals.*

LEFT: *The walls of the garden room were decorated by Vanessa Bell in a grey stenciled design with freehand white flowers. Vanessa's* Self Portrait, *painted in 1958 when she was seventy-nine, hangs to the left of the fireplace. Duncan Grant designed the fish rug in the 1920s, and he painted the figures above the fireplace around 1928.* ABOVE: *Kneeling nude figures above the garden room fireplace were painted by Duncan in 1928; they surround an oval mirror frame that now holds a painted basket of flowers.*

it or redecorated on top of the old. Following Duncan's death, a trust established in 1980 was able to purchase Charleston and begin its restoration. The house had to be stripped to the lathe, the roof replaced, mildew arrested and insects eliminated. The most difficult task was the restoration of the surfaces and objects in the house, with the goal of returning them to their lived-in appearance, not something brand new. Family members took part in the restoration; Angelica Grant painted walls

and Quentin Bell, Vanessa's son, replicated tiles and pottery. The garden was restored and the pond cleared. Finally the house was opened to the public in 1986, restored to the magical, bohemian creativity that makes Charleston such a moving experience today.

Entering the house, the plain, grey walls of the passageways are in surprising contrast to the rich colors in the main rooms. Clive Bell's study, the first room off the entrance hall, is warmly colored with distempered green walls and bold designs, such as large abstract circles painted around the fireplace. Vanessa's simple paintings of flowers around the window still survive from 1916, while Duncan's door panel paintings of a still life (1917) and an acrobat (1958) give the room a lighthearted charm. Furniture includes a pair of comfortable armchairs upholstered in fabrics designed by Duncan and Vanessa.

The dining room, across from Clive's study, is striking with grey-and-yellow abstract designs stenciled on the black walls, all of which were painted over wallpaper. A large round table with its top painted by Vanessa is the center of the room. Meals were served off dishes designed by Grant for Clarice Cliff. A ceramic lampshade made by Quentin Bell hangs over the table.

Vanessa's bedroom, farther along the main hall, was remodeled in 1939 with French windows opening onto the garden. Portraits of Vanessa's friends and family cover the walls, while furniture is a mix of family antiques and pieces embellished with the Bloomsbury Group's bold colors and designs, such as the marvelous screen of abstract figures painted by Duncan in 1913.

OPPOSITE, TOP: *Clive Bell's study has some of the earliest decorations in the house. Vanessa painted the window embrasure in 1916–17, and in front of it is a tiled table by Duncan Grant designed in 1930.* OPPOSITE, BOTTOM: *Vanessa Bell's studio after 1939 was in an attic bedroom. An unfinished plaster bust of Virginia Woolf was made by Stephen Tomlin in 1931 (when she was forty-nine) and* rests on an eighteenth-century Italian chest of drawers. A portrait of Adrian Stephen by Duncan (c. 1910) is on the left. ABOVE: *Clive Bell's study is centered on a colorful fireplace painted by Vanessa with bold circle motifs in 1925–26. The bookcases hold Clive's collection of art books. The armchair is covered in fabric designed by Vanessa ("Abstract").*

ABOVE: *Duncan Grant's studio holds an assortment of objects, much as he kept it when he was alive. He painted the tri-fold screen in the 1920s, and the walnut cabinet (which belonged to the novelist W. M. Thackeray) holds a collection of ceramics decorated by Charleston artists.*
OPPOSITE: *Duncan Grant's studio is centered on the fireplace, painted with florid nude caryatids in 1932. The clutter on the mantel reflects the way Grant maintained the room.*

One of the most striking rooms on the ground floor is Duncan's studio, adjoining Vanessa's bedroom. Added in 1925, the light-filled room is painted in soft tones of grey, green and dark pink to highlight Duncan and Vanessa's paintings. Duncan used the studio as his sitting room in later years. Today the room still looks as if Duncan had just stepped out for a moment—it's filled with a clutter of photographs, cards and mementos, as well as Duncan's brushes and tubes of paint. Muscular youth painted by Duncan surround the fireplace, while his 1934 painting *Male Nude* still rests on an easel in the corner.

Bedrooms, a library and a stark green bathroom enlivened by a painting of a female nude around the tub are on the second floor.

Charleston still echoes with the imagination and talent of the iconoclastic band of artists who made it their home for more than sixty years. As soon as you step inside, you understand why it is still so special today.

Charleston is located approximately 30 minutes by car from Brighton in the picturesque, East Sussex countryside. It is open seasonally and you should call ahead or visit their Website for times: www.charleston.org.uk; telephone: (011 44 1323 811265).

ABOVE: *The walls of the dining room were covered with stenciled wallpaper painted in a geometric pattern by Duncan Grant, Quentin Bell and Angelica Grant in 1939. Done freehand with unstable materials, the look remains fresco-like as the white chalk base reappears through the pigment.*
RIGHT: *The dining room is centered on a large, circular dining table decorated by Vanessa in 1952. Guests around the table over the years included Virginia and Leonard Woolf, E. M. Forster, Maynard Keynes, and T. S. Eliot. Plates were designed by Duncan Grant for Clarice Cliff in 1934.* OPPOSITE: *Vanessa Bell painted the kitchen cabinets with flowers and fruits in the 1950s; the paintings were done on canvas and then attached to the cabinet doors.*

OPPOSITE: *Maynard Keynes was one of Vanessa Bell's most frequent guests. In a bedroom set aside for him is a firescreen made of two wooden panels, painted by Duncan in the 1930s. The only known painting of Charleston by Vanessa, done in* the 1950s, *hangs above the mantel.* ABOVE: *Clive Bell's bedroom features his antique French bed that Vanessa decorated in 1950. The yellow-and-green walls date to 1917, when Vanessa used the room as a studio.*

LEFT: *The green bathroom was originally the only bath in the house, and had only cold water until 1919. The bathtub panel of a reclining nude was painted by Richard Shone in 1970.*
OPPOSITE: *Vanessa Bell's bedroom featured French doors that open directly to the garden. Her French Provincial desk was always cluttered with writing materials. A striking screen painted by Duncan in 1913 for the Omega Workshops divides the room.*

CRAGSIDE

C ragside was built as the country retreat of the first Lord William Armstrong (1810–1900), one of Britain's most successful Victorian inventors. A brilliant scientist, Armstrong was also a successful businessman and was involved in the early science of hydraulics (developing applications from the first power cranes to the engine that raised the Tower Bridge in London in 1894). Armstrong was a gun maker as well, supplying armies and navies throughout Europe with artillery and ironclad warships. He had built Cragside, a modest shooting lodge on a steep slope in the rugged mountains of Northumberland in 1863. But he quickly decided he wanted a more impressive residence, so in 1869 contacted London architect Richard Norman Shaw to expand the house.

Shaw was well known for his romantic houses designed in the Old English style, based on the half-timbered, medieval manor houses and barns of southern England. Shaw slowly transformed Cragside over the next twenty years, remodeling it into a rambling country manor. Furnished with Armstrong's collections of paintings and Arts and Crafts furnishings, the house became a celebrated example of Arts and Crafts design. But Armstrong also used Cragside as a testing ground for many of his inventions, such as hydraulic machines used to turn the spit in the kitchen and provide electricity to light the house (Cragside, in fact, was the earliest house in the world to be lit by electricity generated by water power, in 1878). Hot and cold running water, central heating, telephones, a passenger lift and even a Turkish bath, all installed in the 1880s, earned Cragside the title of "the palace of a modern magician."

The house was built in three phases. A library and dining room were added on to the north end of the house between 1870 and 1872, with Turkish baths beneath and bedrooms above. The second phase, built between 1872 and 1877, included the addition of a first-floor art gallery at the opposite end of the house and at right angles to the front, and this section linked the house to the Gilnockie Tower, which had been on the site originally. Finally Shaw

The two-story, tiled kitchen featured Armstrong's latest inventions, including a hydraulic lift for bringing up pots and pans from the scullery below.

dug farther into the mountainside and added an elaborate drawing room at the southeast corner of the home between 1883 and 1884.

The hillside on which Cragside was constructed was originally barren rocks and boulders. Over the thirty years he lived at the house, Armstrong created five lakes, along with streams and waterfalls, and added more than seven million trees and shrubs, ferns, and heather to the thousand acres surrounding the house, until the entire estate became a heavily forested, scenic wonderland.

The entrance hall, remodeled by Shaw from 1872 to 1874, is highlighted by two Gothic arches—the larger leading to the principal reception rooms and the smaller to the servants' wing. A small lobby with a fireplace was also added to allow visitors to warm themselves from the inclement weather before entering the rest of the house. The servants' wing leads past the butler's pantry to the large two-story kitchen, which was enlarged in 1885. A scullery underneath the kitchen was used for washing pots and pans, which were then taken up to the kitchen by a dumbwaiter lifted by hydraulic power that also was used to turn the kitchen spit. The main dining room and library were the first rooms added by Shaw, in 1870 to 1872, and survive unaltered. The dining room, decorated by Shaw, is centered on a carved stone inglenook and fireplace. The ceiling and wainscoting are paneled in light oak, which give the room a classic Old English atmosphere. A broad set of bay windows looks out upon the gardens and floods the room with light. A large, richly carved Gothic stone arch encloses the inglenook and fireplace, which is carved from Derbyshire Russet marble and boasts corbels carved with cocks and wolves. Luminous stained-glass windows of the Four Seasons on either side of the fireplace were designed by William Morris in 1873. Furnishings include firedogs and settles around the nook designed by Shaw, along with a plate warmer by W. A. S. Benson.

The library was the first room designed by Shaw in 1872 and remained the main living room of the house. Its bay window was built out over the face of the rock and has a commanding view of the glen below. Paneled in light oak to five feet and capped by an intricate beamed and coffered ceiling, the library again evokes the masculine Old English look that Shaw favored. The walls above the paneling are covered in their original embossed paper painted in a rich snuff color. Morris & Company provided stained glass for the windows, with scenes from the life of St. George (originally designed by Rossetti in 1862) and a second series of classic authors (originally designed by Burne-Jones and Ford Madox Brown).

ABOVE: *Half-timbering, ivy-covered stone walls and a red tile roof add to Cragside's Old English charm.* LEFT: *Carpet bedding, popular in the nineteenth century, has been re-created at Cragside in its extensive gardens.*

EAST OR WEST HAMES BEST

A fireplace of Egyptian onyx made by James Forsyth (one of Shaw's favorite craftsmen) is surrounded by blue and white tiles by Alfred Stevens. Ebonized furniture designed by Shaw and made by Gillows of Lancaster includes a set of Queen Anne chairs with caned seats and leather backs decorated with pomegranates and gilt. Armstrong's electric lights powered by an electric generator were made from four large cloisonné enamel vases that were converted into electric lamps.

The study was originally Lady Armstrong's sitting room but became her husband's study shortly after completion. A molded-plaster ceiling, red walls and a gilt cornice make the room rich and inviting. The room is decorated with an early portrait of Armstrong in 1831, along with views of Cragside and Bamburgh Castle, which he purchased in 1891.

Returning to the entrance hall from the study, an imposing hand-carved oak staircase leads to the first floor. The newel posts are guarded by intricately carved sitting lions that

OPPOSITE: *The dining room's stone inglenook and fireplace were designed by Shaw and featured stained-glass windows by Morris of the Four Seasons.* ABOVE: *The opposite end of the dining room, with a large bay window overlooking the gardens. The dining table and chairs are original to the room.*

hold wrought-iron light posts topped with petal shades. Bedrooms upstairs are named by their decorative schemes, including the Yellow, White, Red and Brown bedrooms. The Owl bedroom, set apart from the other bedrooms with a short, separate staircase on the second floor, was used as a guest bedroom and decorated in 1884 for a visit from the Prince and Princess of Wales. Walls are covered with Morris's Venetian paper, and a magnificent black walnut half-tester bed with carved owls at the foot was designed by Shaw. The first-floor gallery, added by Shaw between 1872 and 1877, links the house to the last addition, the opulent

OPPOSITE: The carved oak main staircase is highlighted by carved lion newel posts holding light standards. ABOVE: The library was designed by Shaw in the Old English style, with a carved oak ceiling and wainscoting. Stained-glass windows were by Morris & Company. The room was lit by incandescent electrical lights powered by a hydroelectric generator.

ABOVE: *The Owl bedroom is centered on a half-tester bed with carved owl finials, designed by Shaw in 1884 for a visit by the Prince and Princess of Wales.* OPPOSITE: *The Yellow bedroom is papered in Morris's "Fruit" and was used for visitors (the Armstrongs had no children).*

drawing room. A colorful stained-glass window of birds and butterflies on the landing was supplied by Morris in 1873. Lit by a long expanse of skylights across the top, the gallery's excellent natural light was supplemented by arc lights powered by a hydroelectric generator in 1878, the first electric lighting of this type in the world. Now hung with Armstrong's collection of paintings from the late nineteenth century, including many by H. H. Emmerson, his favorite artist, the gallery was originally designed to display natural history specimens, some of which are still shown in the cabinets.

The gallery leads to the drawing room, built between 1883 and 1884 by Shaw as his most elaborate room in the house. An enormous, two-story inglenook and fireplace fills the entire south wall of the room. Designed by W. R. Lethaby, Shaw's chief assistant, it was carved from Italian marble and weighs ten tons. To protect the marble on the fireplace, smoke was drawn underground to a chimney disguised as a rock pile in the hillside above the house. Art in the room includes a masterpiece of Pre-Raphaelite sculpture, *Undine* by Alexander Munro. Undine was a water nymph who accidentally drowned her errant husband with her embrace.

ABOVE: *The gallery leads to the drawing room and was used as a picture gallery and natural history museum.* RIGHT: *The drawing room was Shaw's most elaborate addition and is centered on the elaborate carved marble inglenook and fireplace that weighs ten tons.*

Armstrong continued adding onto Cragside, having a billiards room and electrical room built in 1895, when he was nearly eighty-five. Lord Armstrong died in 1900 and left £1,400,000 ($2,800,000), but as he had no children or direct heirs, the estate passed to his great-nephew, William Watson-Armstrong. By 1908 Watson-Armstrong had lost most of his fortune in bad investments and sold the best of his uncle's art collection. Cragside remained in the family for another seventy years, until 1977, when the third Lord Armstrong gave the estate and the surrounding parkland to the Treasury, which transferred it to the National Trust. Cragside has remained open to the public since 1979 and has become one of the Trust's more popular houses.

Located in northeastern England, Cragside is one mile north of Rothbury. The best time to visit is during the summer months, when the gardens can be enjoyed. Visit the National Trust's Web site at www.nationaltrust.org.uk and search for "Cragside House, Garden and Estate" for directions and hours of operation. Telephone 01144.1669.620150.

HILL HOUSE

ABOVE: *The gardener's shed at the base of the turret echoes the staircase turret precisely. Mackintosh even included a copy of the front door on the shed.* OPPOSITE: *The south façade of Hill House shows Mackintosh's massing of forms combined with Scottish baronial accents, such as the staircase turret.*

ill House, the family home of prominent Glasgow publisher Walter W. Blackie, was designed by Scotland's Charles Rennie Mackintosh in 1902. Blackie was looking for something other than the traditional English home—he was tired of quaint plaster-and-beamed walls, brick facades and red-tile roofs. Blackie, rather, wanted something unique, a home with grey rough-cast walls and a slate roof, construction that was "honest" with the massing of its parts forming the architecture. It was thus fortuitous that friends recommended him to Charles Rennie Mackintosh, a Glasgow architect already well known for the striking Glasgow School of Art (1897–99). Mackintosh, it turned out, shared Blackie's ideals and desire to create something unique, a blend of the avant-garde with traditional Scottish baronial architecture, "designs by living men for living men."

Before meeting Mackintosh, Blackie had already decided to move from Glasgow to Upper Helensburgh, a small city twenty miles northwest of Glasgow, and had purchased a hilltop lot overlooking the small town and the Firth of Clyde. Mackintosh and Blackie worked well together, even though Blackie's concern about costs as well as aesthetics resulted in several rooms, such as a billiards room and a den, being cut from the plans. Mackintosh designed every detail of the interiors, from the geometric, angular rooms with their abstract friezes of stylized roses, to the striking, ebonized furniture that, in reality, was not at all comfortable. Color was strictly dictated by Mackintosh in each room, a palette of blacks and white, offset by soft greys, pinks and blues. Mackintosh created a unique home, one he described as ". . . not an Italian Villa, an English Mansion House, a Swiss Chalet, or a Scotch Castle. It is a Dwelling House." But it was a home that nonetheless followed the constructs of the Arts and Crafts movement, emphasizing the use of vernacular materials in a regional context and the involvement of the architect in every detail. Mackintosh's goal was to design a home "alive with individuality and revolutionary motive."

Blackie's insistence that the form of the house be traditional was satisfied by Mackintosh's creation—a Scottish castle with small recessed windows, tall angular chimneys and a prominent drum staircase turret built, however, in a new and thoroughly modern vocabulary. The house was made visible from the street, not secluded by plantings or large walls, as Mackintosh felt strongly that architecture should be treated as art and enjoyed by everyone. The west gable gives visitors their first impression of the stark geometry of the craggy home, which is entirely coated in softly colored grey harling (rough cast). The main door is discrete, recessed into the façade and subtly outlined in golden sandstone blocks. The south façade looks out over the sloping lawns and the river and Gareloch below. Recessed, irregular win-

OPPOSITE: *The library, directly off the entrance, was also used for receiving guests. Lined with bookcases, the room is a masculine retreat.*
LEFT: *Walter Blackie, a prominent Glasgow publisher and patron of the local arts, hired Mackintosh to design his new family home in 1902. Blackie wanted something different from the typical cozy English cottage.*

dows emphasize the massing of the gables and the angularity of the home as their placement follows Mackintosh's motto of form following function. A turreted spiral staircase connects the main quarters of the house with the service wing, and a miniature version of the turret is set at its base; designed as a gardener's shed, the smaller structure helping to emphasize the massiveness of the main tower.

The interior of Hill House was methodically thought out by Mackintosh, with symbols of the Blackies' interests carefully expressed in his choice of designs and motifs. In the main vestibule, for example, three small motifs are stenciled of checkered squares cut across with the curving outline of a tulip—an announcement to visitors that they are entering a home in which nature and science are honored equally. To the right of the entrance is the library, which also functioned as a reception room. Lined with dark-stained oak shelves inset with blue and purple glass, the room is a man's domain. Carved motifs above the bookshelves include a tree whose branches bear books, an open book itself and a bird in flight, representing thoughts on the wing, a common motif for places of study. The main hall lies at the top of four stairs beyond the library, protecting it from casual callers. Purposely dim and mysterious, the walls of the hall are paneled in darkly stained pine set between panels of a stylized organic

ABOVE: *A hall clock echoes the rectilinear designs of the home.*
RIGHT: *The main hall was paneled in dark pine inset with panels of an abstract organic frieze. Purposely dark and somber, it was lit by rectangular overhead lights. The motif of squares and rectangles is repeated in the carpet and furniture.*

frieze. An open staircase is enclosed by tall, narrow beams decorated with small insets of colored glass that sparkle like the wings of insects. Large rectangular light fixtures echo the linearity of the hall, and squares and rectangles are repeated as motifs in the carpet, as well as in the oak chairs and table.

The transition from the darkness of the hall to the brightness of the drawing room is like leaving the gloom of the forest for a colorful garden. Bright light floods in from the bank of bay windows across the south end of the room and highlights the ivory walls, decorated with stencils of stylized pink roses separated by silver tree trunks. Meant to suggest an indoor rose garden, the motif of abstract roses is repeated in the pink stained-glass squares in the windows, the stenciled patterns of abstract roses on the upholstered furniture, and even the antimacassars Mrs. Blackie commissioned from Margaret Macdonald Mackintosh of green velvet dripping with blue glass beads. Margaret Macdonald Mackintosh, Mackintosh's wife and an accomplished artist of the period, contributed to the room's design, including a stylized gesso panel above the fireplace of the story of Sleeping Beauty, symbolic, perhaps, of the Blackie fortune, which was derived from the publication of fairy tales. While most of the original furniture of the room has disappeared, an original small cube table of ebonized wood rests in front of the window bay. An elegant writing desk, luxuriously decorated with inlays of mother-of-pearl and designed by Mackintosh for Anna Blackie, was reacquired in 2002 and now rests in the drawing room. Mackintosh's hope was

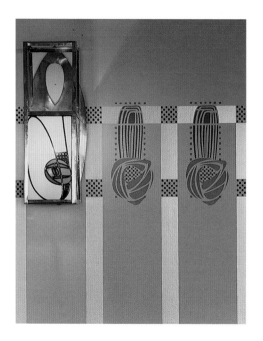

ABOVE: *The drawing room walls are decorated with stylized pink roses on silver trunks. Mrs. Blackie had the wall sconces designed with stained-glass roses.* RIGHT: *An important ebonized writing desk inlaid with mother-of-pearl, made for Mrs. Blackie by Mackintosh, was reacquired for the house in 2002.* OPPOSITE: *The drawing room, opening off the main hall, is awash in light flooding in from the south bay of windows. Decorated in tones of ivory, silver and pink, it is meant to evoke a summer garden.*

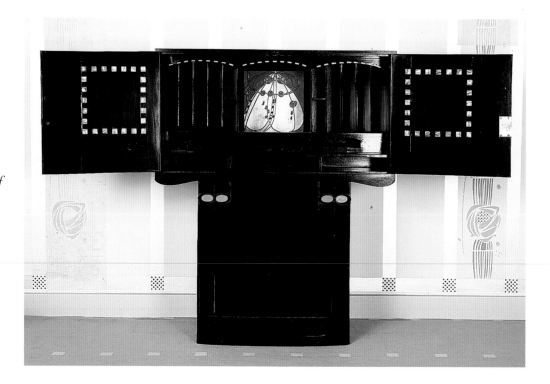

OPPOSITE: *The parlor furniture even has antimacassars of stylized roses with glass petals, commissioned by Mrs. Blackie from Margaret Macdonald Mackintosh. A gesso mural painted by Margaret also highlights the mantel top on the right of the room.*
LEFT: *One of the Blackie family reads in the drawing room in the early 1900s.* BELOW: *Abstract roses are stenciled on the upholstered window seat below the window bay in the parlor.*

that "The message will still be of nature and man, of order and beauty, but all will be sweetness, simplicity, freedom, confidence, and light."

The dining room, next to the parlor, is paneled in dark pinewood and is also a more somber room. Mackintosh designed only the fireplace, with its steel surround and lights, and the overhead stained-glass chandelier. The Blackies used their own traditional dining room furniture to keep costs down.

The first floor is reached by the main staircase, an essay in linear and rectangular forms. A spectacular light fixture of metal cubes inset with deep purple glass lights the landing and echoes the theme of squares found throughout the house. Upstairs, the main bedroom at the southwest corner of the house was Mrs. Blackie's room, connected to Mr. Blackie's via his dressing room. Designed as a rose bower for Mrs. Blackie, stenciled roses are trained up a rose trellis on the walls. The room is L-shaped, and a barrel-vaulted alcove hides the large white carved bed with tall, rose-colored glass cabinets behind. Copies of embroidered hangings by Margaret Macdonald Mackintosh hang across the bed's cabinets. Tall, rectilinear, ebonized ladder-back chairs are elegant accents in the room. Additional bedrooms once used for the Blackie girls have now been turned into administrative spaces.

Hill House is twenty miles northwest of Glasgow, an easy and picturesque drive and also is accessible by rail. Owned by the National Trust of Scotland, be sure to check opening times before you visit: telephone: 011 44 1436 673900; www.nts.org.uk.

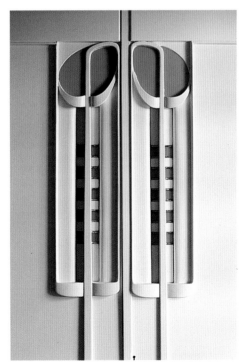

OPPOSITE: *Mrs. Blackie's bedroom contains a white carved bed in a barrel-vaulted alcove lit by a tiny recessed window. The walls are decorated with stenciled roses trained up a trellis.* FAR LEFT: *Mackintosh designed tall, rectilinear ladder-back chairs for Hill House that repeated the geometric patterns found throughout the house. The chairs were not very comfortable, however.* ABOVE: *Silver basins rest on the washstand, which bears a checkerboard motif also used elsewhere in the house.* NEAR LEFT: *Stylized roses with pink stained-glass insets in Mrs. Blackie's bedroom.*

KELMSCOTT MANOR

ABOVE: Morris in the Home Mead *depicts William Morris in the gardens of Kelmscott. Carved by George Jack from a design by Philip Webb, the stone sculpture was made for the pair of Memorial Cottages built by Jane in the village of Kelmscott as a memorial to William Morris in 1902.* OPPOSITE: *Kelmscott Manor's east front. Built of local limestone in the sixteenth century, Kelmscott Manor was enlarged by the addition of another wing on the right around 1670. Stone walls enclose the gardens leading to the front entrance.*

Kelmscott Manor, William Morris's holiday home from 1871 until his death in 1896, was an idyllic country escape and an important source of inspiration for him. Located in the quiet Oxfordshire countryside, the Elizabethan stone building had been built around 1570 by Richard Turner, a local farmer, and enlarged by later generations. Surrounded by walled gardens and sited near the upper reaches of the River Thames, it was the perfect retreat from life in sooty, congested London.

Morris and his family were living at the time in London, on the premises of his company, Morris, Marshall, Faulkner & Co., and Morris was anxious to find a country home with clean air, which he felt to be important for the health of his wife and his two young daughters. Another motive for leasing the manor was his wife Jane's developing affair with Dante Gabriel Rossetti, the painter and poet and a partner in the firm. Divorce was ruled out for fear of social ostracism, so a house in the remote countryside far from London gossip seemed a perfect solution. In a most civilized arrangement, Morris and Rossetti signed a joint lease: Morris was to have use of the home for holidays with his family, and for Rossetti it was an out-of-London studio. Morris settled his wife and their two daughters, May and Jenny—along with Rossetti—into the manor in July of 1871, and then Morris left for an extended trip to Iceland, hoping all would be content.

Rossetti's presence at Kelmscott and his relationship with Morris's wife, however, severely strained his friendship with Morris. Rossetti, in turn, tired of the flat meadowland, which flooded in the winter, and the four-hour journey from London. He became increasingly paranoid and ill-tempered following a mental breakdown in 1872. Although Morris offered to withdraw from the lease, in 1874 Rossetti decided to leave. Morris then engaged his friend and publisher Frederick Startridge Ellis as the new co-tenant of the manor and continued to enjoy Kelmscott's rural beauty for the next two decades, often bringing clients from London to fish in the Thames, even during the winter. As Morris's company was becoming increasingly successful,

especially after 1875 when he took over its sole control, he used his frequent visits to Kelmscott Manor as an important source of relaxation and inspiration. Many of his most popular designs were drawn from his sketches of the gardens and countryside surrounding his beloved retreat. Morris's enthusiasm for the "Old House" is still contagious today. As he wrote in 1895:

> The house from this side is a lowish three storied one with mullioned windows . . . The roofs are covered with the beautiful stone slates of the district, the most lovely covering which a roof can have, especially when, as here and in all the traditional old houses of the countryside, they are "sized down"; the smaller ones to the top and the bigger ones toward the eaves, which gives one the same sort of pleasure in their orderly beauty as a fish's scales or a bird's feathers . . . The garden, divided by old clipped yew hedges, is quite unaffected and very pleasant, and looks in fact as if it were part of the house, yet at least the clothes of it: which I think ought to be the aim of the layer-out of a garden.

One thing to keep in mind if visiting the house is that it has been refurbished with several layers of possessions. When Morris lived there it was a simple holiday home and contained little of his furniture or possessions. It has now been furnished with objects brought from Kelmscott House in London after Morris's death, including furniture made for him by Philip Webb while Morris still lived at Red House (1860–65), some objects collected by Rossetti, and

ABOVE: *An 1893 copy by Charles Fairfax-Murray of Rossetti's 1871 oil portrait of Jane Morris hangs on the bedroom wall.* RIGHT: *Mrs. Morris's bedroom is centered on a four-poster mahogany bed in which William Morris was born in 1834. The walls and bed are decorated with "Willow Boughs," an 1887 design.*

even a few possessions from the Turner family, including the tapestries in the Tapestry Room. Gifts and donations relating to Morris and his family have also accumulated over the years.

Upon entering the house, the narrow, dark screens passage is hung with Morris's Cherwell velveteen curtains, which were designed in 1887. From the screens passage you enter the hall, which, with its low ceilings and its original large fireplace, is cozy and welcoming. The windows are hung with "Strawberry Thief" chintz (1883); now faded, the curtains are thought to have been in place since 1890. A framed embroidery on the wall is of Penelope; worked by Bessie Burden, Jane's sister, it is mounted on green serge and is one of a series designed by Morris for the Red House. The furnishings are simple: a large, round oak table in the center of the room, along with two oak side chairs, which were already in

The Green Room walls are hung with "Kennet," a chintz designed by Morris in 1883. Blue-and-white Morris tiles were used to decorate the original stone fireplace. A seventeenth-century carved oak chair with a book box in the seat was daughter Jenny's chair, and the armchair is upholstered in Morris's 1878 "Bird," a heavy blue wool.

the home in 1870; these are supplemented by several Sussex chairs—small, ebonized occasional chairs with rush seats sold by the Morris firm from 1866 onward.

From the hall one passes through a seventeenth-century oak screen into the lobby. The screen is flanked by an important "Cabbage and Vine" tapestry, woven by Morris himself in 1879, as well as an unfinished embroidered wall hanging of Guenevere, or *La Belle Iseult*, based on an early sketch of Jane before their marriage in 1859. An imposing, ebonized settle with a curved hood and leather panels painted with flowers and a diaper pattern, originally designed by Philip Webb for the Red House and later moved to Kelmscott, rests along the lobby's south wall, while eleven framed charcoal drawings by Edward Burne-Jones of *The Signs of the Zodiac* are hung on the walls. The drawings were sketches for zodiac figures painted on the paneling of the Green Dining Room at the Victoria and Albert Museum in 1866–67. Copper candlesticks by W. A. S. Benson, a ruby luster dish by William De Morgan, and William Morris's overcoat hanging on the back of the door complete the lobby's furnishings.

Through the lobby is the Paneled Room, which has a grander air with its higher ceiling and beautifully carved c. 1670 original stone fireplace. The walls are covered in late-seventeenth-century paneling, painted a simple white, and are accented with plain linen curtains, also white, based on remnants found during restoration of the house in 1964. Furniture includes three easy chairs upholstered in Morris's blue wool "Peacock and Dragon," an ebonized and gilded occasional chair by Philip Webb, and a circular table by George Jack designed for the Morris firm in 1890. Rossetti was fascinated with Jane Morris, as he felt her exotic beauty made her the perfect model, and this is seen in his four drawings and one painting of her hanging in the room. His painting entitled *The Blue Silk Dress*, begun when Jane was twenty-six, and painted between 1866 and 1868, particularly shows her mysterious and sensual

William Morris's bedroom boasts a magnificent seventeenth-century oak four-poster bed covered in hangings embroidered by May Morris in 1891. Jane Morris embroidered the bed cover with floral bouquets and a quote from Morris's poem "A Garden by the Sea."

BELOW: *Covered in eighteenth-century paneling and centered on an original c. 1670 stone fireplace, the Paneled Room is furnished with three easy chairs upholstered in "Peacock and Dragon" woven wool. Rossetti's drawings of Jane decorate the walls.* OPPOSITE: *Visitors first enter the house through the Old Hall, which, with its low ceiling and stone fireplace, gives a cozy and welcoming impression. Morris's popular ebonized Sussex chairs surround an oak table, which was in the house in 1871. The curtains are in "Strawberry Thief" chintz, a pattern registered in 1883. Iznik plates and tiles rest in the corner cupboard.*

allure. Other portraits in the room include pastels of Morris's daughters, Jenny, aged ten, and May, aged nine, drawn by Rossetti in 1871.

From the Paneled Room one passes into the Green Room, whose walls are hung with "Kennet" chintz designed by Morris in 1883. The original late-seventeenth-century fireplace is accented with blue-and-white Morris tiles. A sofa and chair are upholstered with fragments of "Bird," a heavy blue wool designed by Morris in 1878 and first used as a wall hanging for Kelmscott House. An embroidered wool hanging in the window bay is Morris's first attempt to make a textile, in 1857. Titled *If I Can*, it was embroidered by Morris and his maid, Mary Nicholson (Red Lion Mary) for his first apartments in London at Red Lion Square. Other furniture includes a large, round medieval-inspired table designed by Philip Webb for Red House in 1860, tiles by Edward Burne-Jones and lighting by W. A. S. Benson.

Upstairs directly above the Green Room is Mrs. Morris's room. "Willow Boughs," Morris's 1887 pattern of tightly woven willow leaves, was used both in the wallpaper and in

the chintz that drapes the mahogany four-poster bed—Morris's childhood bed in which he was born on March 24, 1834. An 1893 copy of Rossetti's *Water-willow* (an 1871 portrait of Jane Morris) hangs on one wall, and an exquisite Gothic jewel casket designed for Jane by Philip Webb and hand painted by Rossetti and his wife, Elizabeth Siddal (died 1862), rests on the chest underneath.

Across the landing, William Morris's bedroom is centered on a striking four-poster seventeenth-century oak bed. Hung with linens embroidered by May Morris in 1891, the valance displays Morris's poem "For the Bed at Kelmscott." The side curtains were embroidered by May in "Trellis," one of Morris's first wallpaper designs, while Jane embroidered the coverlet in colorful bouquets and a quotation from Morris's poem "A Garden by the Sea." A bookcase by Webb from the library at Kelmscott House contains works by Morris.

The Tapestry Room is above the Paneled Room in the seventeenth-century section of the house, and has a similar original stone fireplace. The paneled walls are hung with seventeenth-century Brussels or Antwerp tapestries depicting the life of Samson. The tapestries were in the house in 1871 when Morris moved in and are thought to have hung there since the seventeenth century. A rectangular library table designed by Webb and originally in Morris's library at Kelmscott House sits in the center of the room, and seating includes one of the adjustable armchairs that became known as the "Morris Chair" and was widely copied in the United States.

Following his death in 1896, Morris was buried close to his beloved Kelmscott Manor, in the village's parish churchyard of St. George. His longtime partner Philip Webb designed the family tombstone in the form of a simply sloping roof divided into four quadrants by the branches of a tree, with room for his wife's and daughters' names.

Jane then moved to Kelmscott Manor permanently, along with her elder daughter, Jenny, who had become disabled due to epilepsy. Jane purchased the house in 1913 along with a little over nine adjoining acres, and following her death in 1914, her daughter May inherited the home. May retired to the home in 1923 and dedicated her last years to preserving Kelmscott Manor as William Morris's home. May bequeathed Kelmscott to Oxford University upon her death in 1938, and Oxford then transferred it to the Society of Antiquaries of London in 1962, which continues to run the home today.

Kelmscott Manor is open to the public from late April until the end of September on Wednesdays and some Saturdays. It is located three miles from Lechlade in Gloucestershire, and there are signs in the village from A417 and A4095 (there is no public transport). Call ahead for reservations at 01144.1367.252486. The Web site also has information, www.kelmscottmanor.co.uk.

PRECEDING SPREAD: *The Tapestry Room is hung with four seventeenth-century Brussels or Antwerp tapestries depicting the life of Samson and thought to be original to the house since the seventeenth century. A rectangular center table was designed by Webb and used in Morris's library at Kelmscott House. Eighteenth-century paneling and the original stone fireplace are still intact.* OPPOSITE: *The seventeenth-century stairs lead to the bedrooms. Light fittings are by W. A. S. Benson.*

RED HOUSE

Red House is arguably the most important Arts and Crafts home in England. The first and only house William Morris ever built. The task of decorating Red House inspired him to form his design firm, Morris & Co., and give definition and meaning to the Arts and Crafts movement. Red House was also the first major project of his close friend Philip Webb, an important architect of the period. Morris lived at Red House only from 1860 to 1865, but the house always remained a fond memory, as those early years there following his marriage were among the happiest of his life. Morris's search for a meaningful course in life, one in which he could contribute to society as well as live a good life surrounded by art and beauty, all began at Red House. His often-quoted motto "Have nothing in your houses which you do not know to be useful or believe to be beautiful" was inspired by his half-decade at the redbrick turreted manor.

When Morris first purchased the land for Red House in 1858, it was still in the rural Kent countryside of Bexleyheath, mostly orchards and farms, yet conveniently located only a short train ride away from central London. Inspired by the medieval architecture of France, which he discovered on a boating trip during the summer of 1858, Morris planned Red House closely with Webb, who understood his romantic ideals but also infused practicality to make the house comfortable and livable. Local redbrick was chosen for the exterior along with red tiles for the roof; the use of vernacular materials would remain a tenet of Arts and Crafts design. The house's L-shaped form followed its function, with two wings meeting in the central, turreted staircase hall. Picturesque details, including turrets, hipped dormers, tall casement windows and bull's-eye windows—asymmetrically placed and some decorated with stained glass—were incorporated.

Morris could not find any contemporary furnishings to suit his taste for a simple Gothic style yet with medieval influences of richly decorated surfaces. So Morris had Webb design everything from the dining room table to the candlesticks and glasses to put on it. The ceilings

ABOVE: *Romantic oriel windows with diamond-glazed panes accent the redbrick front of the house.* OPPOSITE: *Red House viewed from the east shows the inner court centered on a romantic wishing well house topped with an oversized conical roof. The two L-shaped wings meet in the center rectangular staircase turret.*

were painted in abstract geometric patterns that still look quite modern today. Edward Burne-Jones and Webb designed stained glass for the windows, with medieval motifs of barnyard animals and classical maidens, and Burne-Jones was asked to paint murals on the walls based on Greek myths and medieval tales.

Furnishing Red House was so rewarding for Morris that he launched his own decorating company in April 1861, Morris, Marshall, Faulkner & Co., which he later reorganized in 1875 to just Morris & Co., under his sole control. Morris's firm was housed at Red Lion Square in London, and it was the firm's success that made him look for larger quarters by 1865. He considered relocating the company to Red House, and planned an addition that would also house his friend and partner

Edward Burne-Jones and his family. But Burne-Jones backed out of the arrangement, and Morris then decided to move his family back to London to be closer to his work, while also arranging a long-term lease on a house in the Cotswolds—Kelmscott Manor—to provide fresh air for his two young daughters.

Morris never returned to Red House after he left in 1865, as it was too painful for him, but, fortunately, succeeding owners recognized its importance and were able to preserve it without significant changes over the next 140 years. Most of the original furnishings were dispersed, and during World War II the interior was even painted a dark wartime brown. Subsequent owners in the 1950s began restoring Morris's masterpiece, furnishing it with Morris & Co. wallpapers and fabrics. When the last owner died in 2003, Red House was acquired by the National Trust and is slowly being refurbished. A debate continues over whether to furnish the house as it appeared during Morris's occupancy (before he produced most of his famous wallpapers and fabrics) or to use the products of Morris & Co., which would not have been available when Morris resided there.

A redbrick, turreted medieval home is the last thing one would expect to see in Bexleyheath today, an undistinguished, suburban community on the outskirts of congested London. But as you pass through the gates and glimpse steeply pitched redbrick gables rising

OPPOSITE: *The passage, which originally opened to the servants' rooms, is hung with "Cray," a Morris textile named after the valley in which Red House is located. The carved-oak-paneled door at the end leads to a side porch Morris named "The Pilgrim's Rest," after medieval pilgrims who came through the area.* LEFT: *Edward Burne-Jones's stained-glass panel of Fate is set in the center of the window and surrounded by Webb's medieval animals.* BELOW: *Philip Webb painted medieval-inspired animals such as this farmyard goose in the windows of the passage.*

above the trees, you know you have entered a special place. At the front of the house, a pointed, arched brick entryway leads into the entrance hall. Centered on a simple but powerful Gothic oak staircase that is housed in its own square turret, the entrance hall draws visitors into the heart of the home. The walls are papered in a modern reproduction of Morris's 1877 "Apple," and the furniture consists of a massive settle sideboard designed by Webb for the house. Morris hand painted scenes on the settle doors of the legend of King Arthur, with his wife, Jane, and Burne-Jones' wife, Georgiana, as models. Never finished by Morris, the settle was partially covered with brown paint during World War II. The ceilings are hand painted in two different abstract patterns that are still eye-catching today. A glazed screen, on which visitors later inscribed their names, was added in the late nineteenth century to screen drafts from the passage, which to the south of the entrance hall leads to the servants' quarters. Stained-glass windows in the passage were designed by Burne-Jones and Webb, and were based on fifteenth-century motifs of animals and flowers. A reproduction of "Cray," designed by Morris in 1884 (one of his last printed textiles), hangs on the wall of the passage. The passage ends in a small enclosed porch that Morris romantically called "The Pilgrim's Rest," after Canterbury pilgrims who journeyed through the area in the Middle Ages.

Opening off the north end of the entrance hall, the dining room still retains an original dresser designed by Webb for the room. Stained and lacquered in Dragon's Blood Red, it remains an imposing Gothic piece. A canopied settle decorated with floral patterns of

embossed, gilded and painted leather once occupied one end of the room but now is at Morris's country home, Kelmscott Manor. The dining room is papered in Morris's 1879 "Sunflower," and a modern copy of "Golden Lily," an 1897 design by John Dearle (the company's chief pattern designer), hangs in fabric on one wall. An exposed brick fireplace laid in a herringbone design (a popular Arts and Crafts pattern) anchors the room and is decorated with blue-and-white Dutch Delft tiles, one of Morris's favorite designs.

Upstairs, Morris's bedroom awaits refurnishing. Originally its walls were covered with blue serge hangings embroidered by Jane Morris in a pattern of daisies that Morris later reproduced. A large painted wardrobe was designed by Webb for the room and painted by Burne-Jones in scenes from *The Prioress's Tale* in 1857; now it is in the Ashmolean Museum at Oxford. Bull's-eye windows from the corridor overlook the garden below.

OPPOSITE: *The upstairs drawing room is centered on a large settle and bookcase originally designed by Morris while he lived in London and modified by Webb for Red House with a small minstrels' gallery on top. The upper shelves were originally enclosed by three doors that Rossetti painted with scenes from Dante as his wedding gift to William and Jane Morris.* ABOVE, LEFT: *A Gothic dresser designed by Webb for the dining room is still intact and retains its original Dragon's-Blood-Red lacquer finish.* ABOVE, RIGHT: *A simple hanging sconce with heart-shaped cutouts and its original glass shade lights the dresser.*

BELOW: *A gardener glimpsed through a bull's-eye window in the corridor.* RIGHT: *A bull's-eye window in the corridor overlooks the rear court and garden.* OPPOSITE: *Morris's studio on the opposite end of the upstairs corridor is light and airy, its barrel ceiling painted in the abstract pattern of the corridors. The walls are now papered in Morris's 1875 "Marigold."*

Next to Morris's bedroom, the drawing room was the main living area on the first floor. A beamed barrel ceiling extends the room's height into the roof. A large settle-bookcase was designed by Morris in 1856 when he lived in London and adapted for Red House by Webb, who added a playful miniature minstrels' gallery across the top to provide access to the loft at the top of the room. Morris asked Burne-Jones to paint seven wall paintings from *Sir Degrevaunt*, a medieval romance, but only three were completed. A light and airy studio at the opposite end of the corridor was used by Morris for his work, and is now papered in his 1875 Marigold pattern. The studio's ceiling is painted in an abstract design reminiscent of Oriental patterned waves.

The old-fashioned garden surrounds the house, and Morris designed garden and house to work together as one romantic setting, including the original orchard on the north. A medieval well house was placed in the center of the courtyard, supported with heavy oak posts and capped with an oversized conical roof. The garden provided Morris with inspiration for his first wallpaper designs, "Daisy" and "Trellis."

Red House today is about an hour east of central London by car, and is a fifteen-minute walk from the local train station. It is best to book a tour beforehand (telephone 01144.1494.559799) and to verify opening times. For more information, visit www.nationaltrust.co.uk (search Red House).

RODMARTON MANOR

ABOVE: *The gardens are beautifully maintained and complement the house.* OPPOSITE: *The stone terrace at the back of the house.*

Rodmarton Manor, built over a period of twenty years from 1909 to 1929 (work was interrupted from 1914 through 1918 by the war), is one of the best surviving examples of a house truly constructed with local handcraftsmanship following the principles of the Arts and Crafts movement. Built by Claud Biddulph, a wealthy stockbroker, and his wife, Margaret, soon after their marriage in 1906, the house was designed as a large country home that would provide employment for the local villagers and act as a center for the community by supporting and reviving local craftsmanship. Furniture, as well as the house itself, was to be made locally. Rodmarton is considered one of the last great country houses to have been built in England. Homes of this scale became impractical and too costly to maintain as changes swept through English society following the war.

The Biddulphs began by reading books on architecture, including one featuring the work of local Cotswold architect Ernest Barnsley. Impressed by his work, in 1909 the Biddulphs asked him to help design their new home. The well-known architect Sir Edward Lutyens, whose Arts and Crafts domestic designs were considered "fresh and exciting," was an important influence in their planning, so the Biddulphs penciled in their own suggestions on Barnsley's designs. While the first drawings with Barnsley were for a fairly simple house, later plans became much more substantial. Elements such as a large circular courtyard in front of the house, boxwood terraces and extensive walled gardens to the side, and grand public rooms on the ground floor for entertaining were added; even a chapel was included. The house was designed in three wings, each set at an angle to the next: a service wing where the rooms were smaller with lower ceilings, a main living wing where the rooms were higher and larger, and the public reception wing where rooms were spacious and an extra story was added. The house soon grew to 74 rooms, including 19 bedrooms and 622 windows.

After the site for the house was chosen—farmland with a beautiful view towards Marlborough Downs seventeen miles away—a private railroad line was built to haul stone

from a local quarry to the construction site. In the true Arts and Crafts tradition, most of the home was constructed by hand, using very little machinery. Built of warm grey Cotswold stone and tiles, traditional features such as gables, stone mullions, leaded windows, and tall chimneys were included. Local talent was used whenever possible: the local Rodmarton blacksmith made the iron casement windows, and the leaded lights were done by the estate plumber. Keeping in the vernacular tradition, oak trees on the land were felled for the house's timber. Ernest Barnsley's brother Sidney was recruited to design and construct the furniture for the house, as well as his son Edward. Ernest Gimson, another architect working in the Cotswolds, was hired for the plasterwork and furniture design, as well as Peter Waals, a Dutch cabinetmaker who had trained with Gimson. Alfred and Louise Powell, well-known artists for Wedgwood pottery, were asked to paint fur-

ABOVE: *The stone terrace overlooks the gardens.* RIGHT: *Rodmarton is made of local, soft grey Cotswold stone and looks out over the downs. Notice each wing is set at an angle to the next.*

niture and pottery for the house. And Norman Jewson, a local architect who married Barnsley's daughter, designed lead gutters and downpipes decorated with whimsical animals such as owls. The Biddulphs actually began living in the home in 1915, but the final phase of building and furnishing was completed from 1926 to 1929, overseen by Jewson.

The house became not only a family home for the Biddulphs, but a favorite site for local concerts, amateur theatricals, Punch and Judy shows and crafts. The staff consisted of Mrs. Ebsworth, the housekeeper, two housemaids, three parlor maids, one cook and two kitchen maids. The grounds were maintained by six gardeners, and there were also a groom and a chauffeur. In 1940, following the outbreak of World War II, a Catholic school in London was evacuated to Rodmarton; hence, 150 girls and one boy lived in the house during the war. After Mr. Biddulph died in 1954, his son Anthony and his wife, Mary, and their three children moved in. Anthony and Mary soon decided the house was too large, however, and divided the service and main living wings into flats, keeping the public wing for the family. Anthony's son Simon and his wife, Christina, moved back into the house in 1991. The house that we can visit today is the public wing where Simon and Christina continue to live.

The approach to Rodmarton is down Holly Drive, a road bordered on either side by a row of tall, tightly clipped holly and box hedges. The drive leads to a circle in front of the house. Entering Rodmarton, you first come into the long hall, which runs the length of the

ABOVE: *A charming, curved stone balcony adds a romantic touch.* RIGHT: *The lead downspouts were designed by Norman Jewson and decorated with whimsical animals such as owls.*

public wing. Furnished with the original furniture designed for the home when it was built, the hall contains a pair of painted traveling chests designed by Peter Waals and painted in a bright lacquer red with floral designs by Alfred and Louise Powell. A pair of Monk's settles designed by Sidney Barnsley double as seating and storage, as well as tables when their tops are turned horizontally. Other cabinets and wardrobes line the long corridor, most of them made by the Barnsleys, and simple yet striking geometric-patterned rugs were designed by Louise Powell and made by Peggy Lambert (so nicknamed because he had a peg leg). Ancestral portraits of the Biddulph family line the hall.

ABOVE: *A circular drive leads to the main entrance.*

RIGHT: *A pair of red lacquered traveling chests were designed by Peter Waals and painted in a floral motif by Louise and Alfred Powell.* OPPOSITE: *The hall corridor is furnished with chests and wardrobes mostly made by the Barnsleys; the original rugs designed by Louise Powell are still intact.*

The spacious drawing room opens off the hall. Originally sparsely furnished and just used for crafts, the room was given a more sophisticated décor when paneling designed by Alfred Powell was added in 1930. Peter Waals designed several pieces of the furniture in the room, including a pair of walnut writing tables, an oak chest and several tables. Sidney Barnsley made a massive oak chest in the center of the room with protruding dovetails, rounded top and chamfered edges that Margaret Biddulph bought in 1929. Sidney Barnsley also made an oak child's chair called the "punishment chair," as children were punished by having to sit quietly in the chair. The Rodmarton Workshops made simple turned oak lamps for the room. A charming, colorful platter depicting Rodmarton was painted by Alfred Powell, who also designed the upholstered settee.

The drawing room leads into the library, a long room running across the back of the house with beautiful vistas of the gardens. Originally the ballroom, the room was often used for amateur concerts and shows. A striking deep-blue screen was painted by Louise Powell in a delicate floral pattern; a Bluthner piano in the room was also painted by her in the same floral design. Louise Powell also painted several golden lustre pots on the mantel. The beamed oak ceiling is punctuated with simple hanging lamps. Furniture consists of an oak table with a hay-rake stretcher, made by Sidney Barnsley, who also made an oak lamp and bookcases for the room. The Rodmarton Workshops made many of the pieces in the room, including two oak floor lamps, several tables and a macassar ebony armchair.

The drawing room was originally furnished simply, for crafts, but was paneled in 1930. Peter Waals, Alfred and Louise Powell, Ernest Gimson, and the Barnsleys designed furnishings for the room.

The dining room, entered through the library, was only used for guests as the kitchen is some distance away, a design that was not as important when there was no shortage of servants. Sidney and Ernest Barnsley made the dining tables with hay-rake stretchers and double dovetails with diamond detailing on the edges, a decoration also used on the stair railings in the hallway. Brass wall sconces in a floral pattern were designed by Norman Jewson and made by Frank Baldwin.

Upstairs the bedrooms are named after local fields or locations: Little Tarlton, Tarlton Downs, Stonehill and Lordsdown. An oak half-tester bed in Stonehill was made by Sidney Barnsley and the Rodmarton Workshops. The motto of Margaret Biddulph's family is carved over the crest of the half-tester, "*Volvo non valeo*," which translated from Latin means "I am willing but unable." Poole pottery from the 1920s is displayed in the rooms. A large needlework wall hanging of the coronation of King George VI and Queen Elizabeth in 1937 hangs above a dressing table in the Lordsdown bedroom. Made by the Rodmarton Women's Guild, its vibrant design and colors are still striking today.

What makes Rodmarton even more spectacular are the gardens. Opening off the back and west of the house, they are designed in a series of rooms surrounded by walls or hedges, so that a different planting scheme or vista is seen around each corner.

Not far from Kelmscott Manor, Rodmarton is located off A433 between Cirencester and Tetbury in the Cotswolds. Open for tours by appointment, contact Simon Biddulph, telephone: 01285 841253; email: simon.biddulph@farming.co.uk. The Web site is www.rodmarton-manor.co.uk.

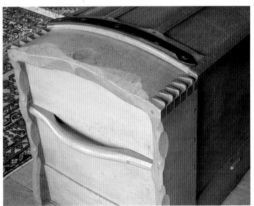

LEFT: *A charger depicting Rodmarton was painted by Alfred Powell.* ABOVE, TOP: *An oak punishment chair for children was made by Sidney Barnsley.* ABOVE, BOTTOM: *A massive oak chest designed by Barnsley sits in the center of the room. Exposed dovetails, rounded top and chamfered edges highlight Barnsley's philosophy of honesty of construction.*

PRECEDING SPREAD: *The library was originally a ballroom and was used for amateur theatrics. A large standing screen, painted by Louise Powell, encloses one end of the room. Sidney Barnsley designed several pieces in the room, including the bookcases and some of the tables.* LEFT: *The handsome folding screen painted by Louise Powell.* BELOW: *A large gold lustreware pot was designed by Louise Powell.* OPPOSITE: *Louise Powell also painted the piano in the same floral motif used on the screen.*

OPPOSITE: *The dining room was only used for guests, as it is not close to the kitchen. The built-in buffet was designed by Sidney Barnsley as was the dining table. The oak chairs are thought to have been made by Scull of Beaconsfield.* LEFT, ABOVE: *The dining table features diamond-carved edges, which are repeated in the stair railings upstairs.* LEFT: *Detail of the stair railings with diamond carving by Sidney Barnsley that matches the dining room table.* ABOVE: *The brass wall sconce was designed by Norman Jewson.*

ABOVE: *Poole pottery from the 1920s rests on a tripod table by Peter Waals in the Tarlton Downs bedroom.* OPPOSITE: *An oak bed in the Stonehill bedroom was made by Sidney Barnsley. The half tester and bedside cabinet were made by the Rodmarton Workshops.*

OPPOSITE: Summertime, *a mural painted in 1924 by Hilda Benjamin, graces the staircase.*
ABOVE: *A large needle-pointed wall hanging of the 1937 Coronation of King George VI and Queen Elizabeth hangs in the Lordsdown bedroom.*

STANDEN

Standen, the home of prosperous London solicitor James Beale, his wife, Margaret, and their family of seven children, was designed by Philip Webb as a comfortable country retreat for their large family. Built between 1892 and 1894, Standen was situated on the site of three rustic farms in the softly rolling hills of southwest Surrey and the Sussex Weald, conveniently a short train ride away from Beale's offices in London. Webb convinced the Beales to incorporate two of the existing farm buildings in the design of their new home, and thus an ancient farmhouse, dating from 1450, and a barn were retained. The picturesque farmhouse had been a yeoman's house in medieval times and was still covered with its original red fish-scale tiles, its roof charmingly overgrown with moss and lichen. The farm buildings were used to form two sides of a grassy courtyard, quaintly called the Goose Green, and Webb used this arrangement as the main entrance to the house—visitors first passed around the old buildings, through a connecting archway and only then came upon the facade. It thus appeared as if Standen had been part of the farm for centuries.

Webb had trained with the eminent Gothic Victorian architect George Edmund Street, and it was while employed in Street's office he first meet young William Morris, who briefly joined the company in 1856. Morris and Webb soon formed a lasting friendship and later a business partnership, but Morris shortly thereafter realized his skills lay more in the decorative arts and left Street's offices to eventually form his own company. Webb continued his architectural career but never built a large practice, instead designing exquisitely detailed Arts and Crafts homes mostly for private clients who could both afford his services and were sympathetic to his strong beliefs on artistic yet practical homes. Webb is quoted as explaining, "I never begin to be satisfied until my work looks commonplace."

Nestled into a slope, the house faced south, with beautiful views over the valley and the Ashdown Forest in the distance. Webb used the preexisting, medieval farmhouse to guide his choice of building materials, choosing local redbrick to tie in with the farmhouse's old red

OPPOSITE: *The east front of Standen, surrounded by gardens and the softly sloping meadows.*
ABOVE: *The gazebo at the south side of the garden overlooking the meadows beyond.*

ABOVE: *Arthur Melville's watercolor of Standen from the garden front was painted in 1896 and hangs in the business room (used by Mr. Beale as his office).* OPPOSITE: *The staircase hall is marked by unusual cutout balustrades designed by Webb after seventeenth-century examples. Generous shelves on the landings are used to display a pair of Pilkington blue green vases and a bronze bust of a young girl.*

tiles, along with a creamy yellow-grey sandstone that was quarried on-site. Webb added roughcast—a mixture of lime, small broken stones, river pebbles and Russian tallow—over the upper levels of the brickwork to minimize water penetration. A five-bay block was designed for the ground level facing the gardens, with tall six-over-three windows housed in round-headed sashes affording views in three directions.

The first floor was hung with red tiles, and the second floor overhung the first to provide shade for the bedrooms below. A large tiled roof punctuated with tall, projecting chimneystacks capped the home. Webb added a rectangular tower to hold two large water tanks and also designed a viewing platform on its roof.

Conservatories were popular for country houses by the late nineteenth century, and Webb included a long, low glass house across the southwest front of the house, overlooking the gardens.

No detail was too small for Webb's concerns—he designed everything from the flooring in each room to the chimneypieces, each one different. John Pearson and W. A. S. Benson, the managing director of Morris & Co. after Morris's death in 1896, made the lighting fixtures following Webb's designs, including dining room wall sconces of large copper repoussé panels

of sunflowers from which dangled delicate glass light bulbs—covered by opalescent glass shades. Webb designed many fitted cabinets, dressers, wardrobes and shelves throughout the house to meet the practical needs of the family and staff. Webb selected his friend William Morris's wallpapers for most of the rooms as well as for the curtains and wall hangings.

Furniture was a mixture of Morris & Co.'s simple pieces, such as rush-seated Sussex chairs and their more traditional Sheraton and Chippendale-style cabinets, along with two elegant rosewood bedroom sets by Collison & Lock. Today Standen also contains ceramics collected by the first administrator, Arthur Grogan, and include an admirable collection of Arts and Crafts potteries, including William De Morgan, Della Robbia, Elton Ware and the Barnstaple potteries.

Standen remained a country retreat for the Beale family for the next seventy years. James Beale died in 1912 and his wife, Margaret, ran Standen until her death in 1936, after which two of their daughters, Maggie and Helen, continued to care for the home. Helen began negotiations to leave Standen to the National Trust before her death in 1972, recognizing its importance as one of the last remaining large homes designed by Webb, but this may not have occurred if it were not for Arthur and Helen Grogan, who came forward and donated a large sum for a long lease of the house, acting as its first administrators. The Grogans were responsible for locating sympathetic furnishings to replace and supplement what was missing, and were the impetus behind Standen's successful reemergence as an icon today of the Arts and Crafts movement.

One enters Standen through a brick porch, paneled in oak with a barrel ceiling and exposed wooden beams, a tribute to Webb's emphasis on honesty of construction, a strongly held belief of the Arts and Crafts philosophy. From the porch, one enters the hall, which was enlarged in 1898 with the addition of a window alcove for a piano, as the Beales often used the hall for teas and musical entertaining. A piano made in 1903 by C. R. Ashbee now rests in the alcove, its keyboard enclosed with doors after a design by M. H. Baillie Scott— and its oak cabinet—inlaid with banding, medallions and delicate floral enamel plaques. Other furniture includes occasional tables and chairs by Morris & Co. that are covered in Morris's stamped velveteens and woven fabrics. The lighting, including hanging electric lamps and brass table lamps, was designed by W. A. S. Benson, with opalescent glass shades by Powell of Whitefriars.

Through the hall is the billiards room, which was also enlarged in 1898. George Jack, Webb's chief assistant, added paneling and bookshelves in 1907. The room is centered on the billiards table, which is lit by three hanging lamps by W. A. S. Benson with pleated green silk shades. Benson also designed the other table lamps and wall bracket lights in the room. Morris's "Compton" chintz covers the windows, and pictures include four chalk drawings by Henry Stacy Marks of The Seasons. Framed panels of tiles by William De Morgan, a pair of

PRECEDING SPREAD: *The drawing room is anchored by a hand-knotted original William Morris carpet (donated by the Royal Oak Foundation). Furniture is mostly by William Morris and includes "Connaught" easy chairs. The walls are papered with Morris's 1879 "Sunflower." Ceramics include examples by William De Morgan and Mark Marshall.* OPPOSITE: *An alcove on the south side of the drawing room looks over the garden and fields beyond. The fireplace and paneling in each room was designed by Webb.* ABOVE: *A pair of tapestry panels of "Tulip and Rose," c. 1876, by Morris, hang on either side of the fireplace in the drawing room.*

Burmantofts turquoise vases and a grotesque toad spoon warmer, an Elton Ware "tyg," or three-handled loving cup, and a ruby and pink lustre bowl decorated by William De Morgan are some of the Arts and Crafts ceramics in the room. A corridor leads to the conservatory, which overlooks the rear gardens and countryside beyond; bougainvillea, oleander and plumbago continue to thrive in the sunny room.

The drawing room is also on the south side of the house and has the best views of the garden. Large copper repoussé fireplace cheeks were designed by Webb and made by John Pearson, C. R. Ashbee's Guild of Handicraft's senior metalworker, in a pattern of intertwining sunflowers. The walls are covered in a combination of paneling, painted white, and the soft pastel greens of Morris's 1879 "Sunflower" wallpaper. A beautiful hand-knotted wool carpet designed by J. H. Dearle and made at Merton Abbey now covers the floor. Lighting by Pearson and Benson includes wall sconces with a sunflower motif and glass shades by Powell of Whitefriars. Furniture in the room was mostly made by Morris & Co., and includes "Connaught" easy chairs still upholstered in their original green stamped mohair, a "Jacobean" armchair designed by E. W. Godwin, and a rosewood armchair and cabinet by Collison & Lock. More Arts and Crafts ceramics displayed in the room include several vases and bowls by William De Morgan, as well as a Martin Brothers gourd vase and a pair of Doulton jars by Mark V. Marshall.

The dining room on the southeast side of the home also overlooks the gardens and is entered through the entrance hall. The paneling is painted in its original Aesthetic green, which sets off a collection of blue-and-white Chinese porcelain that was much in vogue during the

OPPOSITE: *A raised alcove at the end of the billiards room was for watching the game being played. Hanging pool lights were designed by Benson.* ABOVE: *A panel of William De Morgan tiles is framed in the billiards room.*

OPPOSITE: *The dining room mantel was used to display the Beale's blue-and-white Chinese porcelain. The repoussé steel fireplace cheeks were made by John Pearson after Webb's design.*

ABOVE: *The paneling and fireplace in the dining room are painted their original Aesthetic green. The table and Queen Anne chairs were made by S. & H. Jewell & Co. for the room in 1896.*

Aesthetic movement. The handsome paneled fireplace is accented with a pierced, carved panel across its top. S. & H. Jewell & Co. made the dining table and chairs, carved from Spanish mahogany and based on eighteenth-century models, and Margaret Beale, along with several other women in the family, embroidered the chair seats from designs by the Royal School of Art Needlework. The woven wool curtains are Morris's "Peacock and Dragon" (1878).

The morning room corridor leads from the dining room and the entrance hall to the morning room. Facing east, it receives the morning sun and was a favorite spot for the women of the house to gather after breakfast to work on their embroidery and correspondence. Wall hangings of "Daffodil" chintz (1891) have been re-created, and cushions in the room are covered in "Crown Imperial" and "Evenlode" Morris fabrics. An oval mahogany center table designed by Webb for Morris & Co. rests in the center of the room. Comfortable chairs include a Morris adjustable chair and a Sunbury armchair. Pottery includes a collection of Della Robbia vases and chargers, including one by Harold Rathbone, founder of the pottery.

The staircase leading upstairs opens off the main entrance hall and features Webb's unusual, flat balustrades based on seventeenth-century designs. An impressive collection of William De Morgan pottery is displayed on the landings. Walls papered in Morris's 1892 "Bachelor Button," were varnished in 1906 to help preserve the paper. A tapestry of St. Agnes woven in 1887 by Morris based on a Burne-Jones stained-glass design hangs on one upper corridor wall. An 1887 cartoon by Ford Madox Brown called *The Baptism of King Edwin* was one in a series of sketches for twelve paintings illustrating the history of Manchester in Alfred Waterhouse's *Manchester Town Hall.*

The morning room was used by the women of the house to embroider and write letters in the morning sunlight. The walls are hung with a reproduction of Morris's "Daffodil" chintz. The oval center table, designed by Webb, was made by Morris & Co.

The twelve bedrooms on the first floor were used by the Beales, their older children and guests, while the nine bedrooms on the second floor were for the servants and younger children. There was but one bathroom per floor, however, as hip baths and commodes were expected to be used in the individual rooms. Three bedrooms are now open to the public. The Larkspur bedroom, the eldest daughter Amy's room, was papered in "Larkspur" and furnished with several pieces by Ernest Gimson, the Arts and Crafts designer who established his own workshop in the Cotswolds in 1895. The Westbourne bedroom was used by Margaret Beale as her embroidery studio, and is papered in Morris's "Willow Boughs." The north spare bedroom is papered with Morris's "Powdered" (1874) and features intricate wall hangings based on Morris's "Acanthus" that were embroidered by Margaret Beale and her daughters in silk and worsted wool.

The gardens were typical of the Arts and Crafts period, with the use of local materials for formal elements and naturalistic plantings in between. Yew hedges, a trellis and pergolas helped define different garden areas that were carefully blended into the surrounding meadows and landscape. A garden terrace across the south of the house, the quarry gardens (created from the quarry begun for building stone), a bamboo garden, a rose garden and a croquet lawn were created. Well maintained by Mrs. Beale and her daughters, many of the original plantings still survive.

Two miles south of East Grinstead, Standen is a ninety-minute drive south from London. Call for opening times and directions: telephone: 01144 1342 323029, or view the Web site: www.nationaltrust.org.uk/places/standen.

ABOVE: *A Benson table lamp in the Willow bedroom; the wallpaper is Morris's "Willow Boughs."* BELOW: *An original carpet in the north bedroom was woven in Morris's 1875 "Tulip and Lily" pattern by Kidderminster.* OPPOSITE: *An intricate silk-and-worsted-wool wall hanging embroidered by Margaret Beale and her daughters hangs in the north bedroom.*

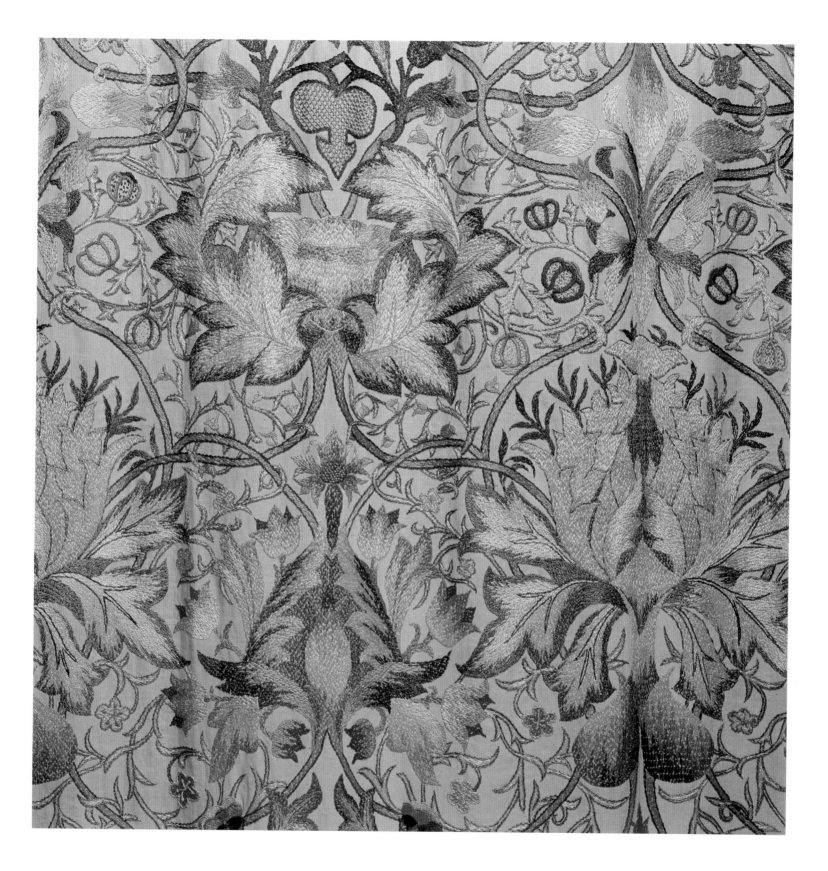

WIGHTWICK MANOR

Wightwick Manor, built for paint manufacturer Theodore Mander between 1887 and 1888, was designed by architect Edward Ould of Liverpool. Ould was well known for his half-timbered, Old English construction, a style that had been first popularized by Richard Norman Shaw in the 1860s. Ould used a mixture of materials, timber framing with plaster, tiles, stone and redbrick, along with irregular windows and complicated multi-gabled roofs, to give Wightwick an idiosyncratic charm and appearance of age. Details were deliberately kept quaint and old-fashioned, such as small windows in the brick chimneystack, an owl and a bat carved on the front porch, even inspirational quotes inside and out. The house, however, was built without guest rooms, and by 1892 it was already too small for the Manders, who now had four children. Ould was called back to design an addition and a new wing was added, centered on an impressive two-story great parlor, a billiards room, dining room and five guest rooms.

Theodore Mander firmly believed in the tenets of the Arts and Crafts movement, and made certain to furnish his manor with the latest, most artistic Arts and Crafts products available, with many of the wallpapers, textiles and furniture ordered from William Morris's firm, Morris & Co. As a wealthy manufacturer, Mander was in the position to afford them. Thirteen rooms were papered with Morris papers, and many of the bedrooms were named after their individual patterns—Pomegranate, Honeysuckle, Daisy. But comfort was as important as beauty, and Wightwick was designed with the latest conveniences, including central heating, electricity and even a Turkish bath. Charles Eamer Kempe, a well-known stained-glass artist of the nineteenth century, was hired to make intricate stained-glass panels for the entrance hall and also oversaw the decoration of the great parlor after its construction.

Theodore Mander died in 1900, aged just forty-seven, and Wightwick was inherited by his eldest son, Sir Geoffrey Mander, and his second wife, Rosalie Gynn Grylls, a writer and Pre-Raphaelite expert. Together they began assembling an outstanding collection of Pre-Raphaelite

RIGHT: *Details such as half-timbering and oriel windows on the upper gable give the house an Old English look.* OPPOSITE: *The main entrance of Wightwick.*

artists, including D. G. Rossetti, J. E. Millais, William Holman Hunt and Edward Burne-Jones. Sir Geoffrey and Lady Mander decided to give Wightwick to the National Trust in 1937 (the first house to be donated to the Trust under its Country Houses Scheme) but continued to add important Arts and Crafts ceramics, stained glass and carpets. While descendants of the family continue to use the family apartments in the home today, Wightwick's interiors were never significantly altered, and it remains one of the best extant examples of original Arts and Crafts decoration as it was interpreted more than a century ago.

Set amongst similar, large homes in an affluent suburb of Wolverhampton in central England, Wightwick is a pleasant surprise of half-timbered, projecting bays; tall, decorative chimneys; and details such as oriel windows and quotes from Shakespeare carved on the gables. The entrance hall, raised one step from the passageway, is centered on a cozy, carved stone inglenook with rich green De Morgan tiles surrounding the fireplace. Seventeenth-century oak paneling was reused from the original old manor house on the site, and a window seat is covered in Morris's "Peacock and Dragon" woven wool. Morris's "Bird" woven wool covers the wing chair in the corner. Magnificent stained-glass windows by Kempe,

RIGHT: *Rows of topiary in the gardens have been beautifully restored.* OPPOSITE: *The entrance hall alcove was also used as a sitting room and features ornate stained-glass windows by Kempe.*

dated 1888, sparkle on the upper sashes of the diamond glazed windows, and represent fortitude, abundance, peace, industry, joy and temperance (the Manders were teetotalers).

The drawing room, which opens off the main hall, faces south and west to capture the afternoon sunlight and best views. It was used by the ladies of the house for teas and afternoon musicals; Mrs. Mander could discreetly escape via a secret door in the fireplace paneling that hides a staircase leading to her private sitting room. Richly furnished, the drawing room features an ornate, Jacobean-style plaster ceiling and an Italian Renaissance carved alabaster fireplace inset with William De Morgan tiles. A quote from John Ruskin is carved in the paneling above. Original c. 1893 William Morris "Dove and Silk" wool-and-silk wall hangings are still on the walls but have faded from their original striking pink and indigo blue. Original light fittings include a pair of chandeliers made by Holman Hunt for W. A. S.

Benson. More Morris fabrics include seat cushions in now-faded blue cotton "Tulip" and upholstery in "Flower Garden" green wool and silk. Stained-glass windows by Kempe illustrate the Annunciation and the Four Seasons. Pre-Raphaelite paintings include a portrait of Jane Morris by Rossetti that was completed by Ford Madox Brown (he added her red hair), a chalk portrait by G. F. Watts, a chalk and wash picture by Ruskin, and a watercolor of Kelmscott Manor by Morris's daughter May. Ceramics include a large jar decorated with dolphins by De Morgan and ruby lustreware dishes painted with stags, goats and pelicans. A large, nineteenth-century Turkish Isnik jardinière was owned by De Morgan and was one of his sources of inspiration. Furniture is mostly eighteenth- and nineteenth-century Dutch marquetry, along with a Regency sofa table and an elbow chair by Morris & Co.

LEFT: *The center of the house, the great parlor, is modeled after a medieval great hall with a polychrome timber ceiling and is furnished with a mixture of Morris & Co. and seventeenth- and eighteenth-century pieces.* ABOVE: *Burne-Jones's painting* Love Among the Ruins *anchors one end of the great parlor and is considered one of his finest works.*

OPPOSITE: *The dining room is paneled with unpolished walnut and has an ornate plaster frieze and ceiling. Morris & Co. fabrics were used for the drapes, and a Morris & Co. hand-knotted rug was* added. ABOVE: *The oak room is the principal visitor's bedroom and carries through the medieval theme from the great parlor.*

RIGHT: *Detail of original "Honeysuckle" wall hangings and four-poster bed hangings.*
OPPOSITE: *The Honeysuckle bedroom is named for the original Morris & Co. "Honeysuckle" wall hangings.*

The library was originally the dining room until the 1893 addition yet still has an Old English feel with oak bookcases and a ribbed oak ceiling. Tiles from Maw's Anglo-Persian designs line the fireplace. Original Morris "Larkspur" remains on the walls, while "Bird and Vine" curtains and a sofa cover were added in the 1940s. Sir Geoffrey Mander added 1870 Morris & Co. stained-glass panels of Milton by Ford Madox Brown and Horace by Burne-Jones in 1947. Armchairs covered in Oriental carpets are mixed with earlier pieces; leather-upholstered chairs from 1660; and oak tables, chairs and a bureau from the seventeenth and eighteenth centuries.

Farther down the hall, the great parlor was added in 1893 as the main room of the home and was meant to give the impression of a fifteenth-century medieval hall. A screens passage entrance highlighted by molded and carved ogee arches; a minstrels' gallery on the second floor overlooking the main hall; an open, timbered roof decorated with Gothic tracery; a bay window filled with armorial glass; and a large inglenook fireplace all gave the impression that the room was centuries old.

Modern touches were acknowledged however—the room's date "1893" is carved above the fireplace, and radiators are concealed behind grilles in the paneling to keep the room warm. Placed at the center of the house, the great parlor was the main passage from the drawing room

to the dining room as well as accessing the staircase to the guest bedrooms. Decorated by Charles Kempe, the room glows with rich fabrics and carpets, stained glass, and tiles. The oak inglenook fireplace is inset with Dutch tiles and has an elaborately carved design of roses highlighted in red, green, gold and black. A colored plaster frieze of the story of Orpheus and Eurydice runs around the top of the room, and the arched roof timbers are also painted in corresponding colors. Panels of Morris's woven wool "Diagonal Trail" are hung below the frieze. Lighting is by George Jack of Morris & Co. with chandeliers by Benson. Original Morris & Co. "Acanthus" wallpaper still hangs in the alcove of the bay window, although the "Tulip and Rose" wool curtains are later additions. Stained-glass windows by Kempe are of appropriately medieval subjects, Saint George, Saint Andrew and Saint Patrick. The room is anchored on the far end by Burne-Jones's 1894 painting *Love Among the Ruins*, considered one of his finest works. Seventeenth-century chairs and tables are combined with a Georgian-style wing chair from Morris & Co. covered in their "Strawberry Thief" cotton and a sofa in "Bird" woven wool.

Through the great parlor, the billiards room was meant for the gentlemen of the house, but ladies were invited to play on occasion. Morris's "Pimpernel" wallpaper was added in 1937 and complements the "Tulip and Rose" and "Bird" woven-wool curtains. A high-backed chair with its original upholstery is attributed to C. F. A. Voysey.

The dining room was designed to face east to avoid the afternoon sun, felt to be disagreeable for dining. The dining room was also placed as far away as possible from the kitchen so that any disagreeable cooking odors would not be noticed. Hot plates and heated serving dishes were used by the servants to keep the food warm in a screened-off hatch; it was not considered proper to view a meal until it was actually placed in front of the diner. Rich, unpolished walnut paneling and an intricate strapwork plaster frieze and ceiling with molded, ribbed pendants designed by Shuffrey give the room a warm, masculine feel. Morris & Co.'s woven wool "Peacock and Dragon" curtains hang on the windows and are complemented by a hand-knotted, vegetable-dyed Morris wool carpet, c. 1900 (acquired in 1961). The chandelier is identical to the one in the drawing room made by Holman Hunt. Art-work includes portraits by Ford Madox Brown of his family, a Holman Hunt portrait of his daughter Gladys, a red chalk profile of a girl by Burne-Jones and a pastel by Rossetti. The Georgian-style chairs are thought to be from Morris & Co., who also provided green glassware by Powells.

The visitor's staircase leads to the guest rooms upstairs, each named for the pattern of Morris paper and fabric on the walls. The Honeysuckle Room is hung with its original Morris "Honeysuckle" printed cotton from 1893. An 1890 Morris hand-knotted rug in the "Small Barr" pattern was added in 1952. The paneled fireplace is tiled with red lustre tiles from Maw, and a quotation from Browning adds an appropriately literary note. Pictures by

ABOVE: *Book illustrator Cecil Aldin designed a frieze of scampering dogs for the night nursery.* OPPOSITE: *The nurse slept with the younger children in the night nursery.*

Burne-Jones, Millais, Simeon Solomon, Spencer Stanhope and Evelyn De Morgan are hung around the room. Furniture includes Morris & Co.'s simple Sussex chairs that belonged to Violet Hunt, the daughter of painter Alfred Hunt, and an oval-seated Rossetti chair also by Morris & Co., which was purchased by Mrs. Mander. The bed hangings were embroidered by May Morris.

The Oak Room was the main visitors' suite and continued the great parlor's medieval theme with an oak-ribbed barrel roof. It is now used to display Morris textiles and Pre-Raphaelite painted furniture collected by the Manders. A large cabinet and cupboard, and folding bed were bought in 1939 from friends of

ABOVE: *Early-twentieth-century toys in the day nursery.* RIGHT: *The day nursery, looking toward the fireplace and window.*

Rossetti and features four scenes from *St. George and the Dragon* stained-glass designs, along with mirrors adapted from Rossetti's 1857 designs for the Oxford Union murals.

The day and night nurseries were placed next to the main bedrooms, an unusual arrangement for the nineteenth century, when children were usually placed in a separate wing or floor. The day nursery was redecorated in 1932 with green walls accented by yellow woodwork and furniture and has been restored to this scheme. The curtains, screen and cushions are from 1929 Voysey designs of "The House Jack Built" and "Alice in Wonderland." Furniture is mostly from the 1880's, repainted yellow in the 1930s. The night nursery was used by the nurse for her bedroom, and the younger children slept here as well until they grew older. The room has been restored to its 1908 appearance and includes a printed frieze of birds and animals by book illustrator Cecil Aldin.

The kitchen, basically unaltered since 1888, still has its original range and cooking utensils. Overlooking the front entrance to the home, it was considered to be in an unfortunate location as the room receives the full afternoon sun during afternoon meal preparations.

The surrounding seventeen acres of gardens were mostly planned in 1904 and 1910, dividing the grounds into gardens around the house, which had strong architectural frameworks of terraces and stone walls, topiary and yew hedges, and formal lawns. Beyond the house the grounds become more informal with banks of shrubs and trees, streams, and pools that merge into the surrounding woodlands.

Wightwick is located in Wolverhampton, north of Birmingham in central England. A National Trust property, visit their Web site to check on opening hours and directions: www.nationaltrust.org.uk, or telephone directly: 01144 1902 760 100. ❧

The kitchen is virtually unchanged with its original and still-functioning range. Walls are tiled for sanitation, an important consideration in the late nineteenth century.

PHOTOGRAPHY CREDITS

Duncan McNeill Photography with Permission by Simon Biddulph: pages 92–111.

National Trust of England: pages ii, 18–29, 44–55, 80–91, 112–145.

National Trust of Scotland, pages 56–67.

Blackwell and the Lakeland Arts Trust, pages 8–17.

Charleston Trust, pages 30–43.

Kelmscott Manor, pages 68–79.

TO VISIT THE HISTORIC HOMES

Blackwell House is located at Bowness on Windermere in the picturesque Lakes District. Call or visit the website for opening times and directions: 01144 15394 46139; www.blackwell.org.uk

Castle Drogo is located in southwest England in Devon. It is a National Trust property. Visit their Web site for opening times and directions: www.nationaltrust.org.uk. Telephone: 011 44 1647 433306.

Charleston is located approximately 30 minutes by car from Brighton in the picturesque, East Sussex countryside. It is open seasonally and you should call ahead or visit their website for times: www.charleston.org.uk; telephone: (011 44 1323 811265).

Cragside, located in northeastern England, is one mile north of Rothbury. The best time to visit is during the summer months, when the gardens can be enjoyed. Visit the National Trust's Web site at www.nationaltrust.org.uk and search for "Cragside House, Garden and Estate" for directions and hours of operation. Telephone 01144.1669.620150.

Hill House is twenty miles northwest of Glasgow, an easy and picturesque drive and also is accessible by rail. Owned by the National Trust of Scotland, be sure to check opening times before you visit: telephone: 011 44 1436 673900; www.nts.org.uk.

Kelmscott Manor is open to the public from late April until the end of September on Wednesdays and some Saturdays. It is located three miles from Lechlade in Gloucestershire, and there are signs in the village from A417 and A4095 (there is no public transport). Call ahead for reservations at 01144.1367.252486. The Web site also has information, www.kelmscottmanor.co.uk.

Red House today is about an hour east of central London by car, and is a fifteen-minute walk from the local train station. It is best to book a tour beforehand (telephone 01144.1494.559799) and to verify opening times. For more information, visit www.nationaltrust.co.uk (search Red House).

Rodmarton is located not far from Kelmscott Manor, off A433 between Cirencester and Tetbury in the Cotswolds. Open for tours by appointment, contact Simon Biddulph, telephone: 01285 841253; email: simon.biddulph@farming.co.uk. The Web site is www.-rodmarton-manor.co.uk.

Standen is located two miles south of East Grinstead, a ninety-minute drive south from London. Call for opening times and directions: telephone: 01144 1342 323029, or view the Web site: www.nationaltrust.org.uk/places/standen.

Wightwick is located in Wolverhampton, north of Birmingham in central England. A National Trust property, visit their Web site to check on opening hours and directions: www.nationaltrust.org.uk, or telephone directly: 01144 1902 760 100.

RESOURCES

AD Antiques

PO Box 2407, Stone, Staffordshire ST15 8WY
Telephone: +44 0 7811 783518
Website: www.adantiques.com
Pottery and ceramics, metalwork, other decorative arts

Art Furniture

158 Camden St., London NW1 9PA
Telephone: +44 0044 207 267 4324
Website: www.artfurniture.co.uk
E-mail: arts-and-crafts@artfurniture.co.uk
Extensive collection, works by Liberty & Co., Shapland & Petter, Heals, Wylie, Lochead, Baillie-Scott, E. A. Taylor, George Walton, more

Arts and Crafts Antiques

Manchester, Northwest UK
Telephone: +44 0161 945 7775
Website: www.artsandcraftsantiques.com
E-mail: David@artsandcraftsantiques.com
Specializing in golden oak furniture, other items also stocked

The County Seat

Huntercombe Manor Barn,
Nr Henley on Thames, Oxon RG9 5RY UK
Telephone: +44 1491 641349 Fax: +44 1491 641533
Website: www.thecountyseat.com
Architect designed furniture from the 19th and 20th centuries, related Art pottery, metalwork and glass

Crafts Nouveau

112 Alexandra Park Road,
Muswell Hill, London N10 2AE
Telephone: +44 0 20 8444 3300
Website: www.craftsnouveau.co.uk
E-mail: lauriestrange@msn.com
Quality furniture and decorative items of the Arts and Crafts and Art Nouveau periods

Glasgow Style

Glasgow, Scotland
Website: www.glasgow-style.co.uk
E-mail: enquiries@glasgow-style.co.uk
Specialize in Scottish pottery and Glasgow Girls ceramics, large selection of other items

Hill House Antiques & Decorative Arts

PO Box 17320, 18 Chelsea Manor Street,
London SW3 2WR UK
Telephone: +44 0 7973 842777
Website: www.hillhouse-antiques.co.uk
Metalware, ceramics, small furniture, pictures and prints, more

The House 1860-1925

On-line furniture store, based in Monmouth, extensive stock
Website: www.thehouse1860-1925.com

Mark Golding

25A Clifton Terrace, Brighton, Sussex BN1 3HA
Telephone: +44 0 1273 327774 / +44 0 7775 535453
Website: www.achome.co.uk
E-mail: mark@achome.co.uk
Morris wallpapers and fabrics, items by Voysey, Dresser, Godwin, Pugin, de Morgan, more

Paul Reeves

32B Kensington Church Street, London W8 4HA UK
Telephone: +44 0 207 937 1594
Fax: +44 0 207 938 2163
Website: www.paulreeveslondon.com
Comprehensive selection of Arts and Crafts antiques, also loan to museums

Puritan Values at the Dome

The Dome, St. Edmunds Rd.,
Southwold, Suffolk IP18 6BZ
Telephone: +44 0 1502 722211
69 Kensington Church St., London W8 4BG
Telephone: +44 0 207 937 2410
Website: www.puritanvalues.co.uk
E-mail: Sales@puritanvalues.com

Remains To Be Seen

62 Wyle Cop, Shrewsbury, Shropshire SY1 1UX
Telephone: +44 0 1743 361560
Website: www.remainstobeseen.co.uk
E-mail: noovo@tiscali.co.uk
Quality furniture and decorative items of the Arts and Crafts and Art Nouveau periods

Strachan Antiques

40, Darnley St., Pollokshields,
Glasgow, G41 2Se Scotland
Telephone: +44 0 141 429 4411
Website: www.strachanantiques.co.uk.com
Comprehensive selection of Arts and Crafts furniture

C20 Twentieth Century Fires

2nd floor, Blankley House, Blankley St.,
Levenshulme, Manchester M19 3PP UK
Telephone: +44 0161 225 1988
Fax: +44 0161 225 6466
Website: www.c20fires.co.uk
E-mail: sales@c20fires.co.uk
Original and reproduction fireplaces, inserts, stoves, surrounds, and tiles

Al Bar-Wilmette Platers

127 Green Bay Road, Wilmette, IL 60091
Telephone: 866-823-8404, 847-251-0187
Fax: 847-251-0281
Website: www.albarwilmetteplaters.com
E-mail: info@albarwilmette.com
Restoration/repair/refinishing of antique hardware and metal fixtures, refurbish locks, large selection of salvage door hardware and light fixtures

Architectural Antiques

1330 Quincy St. NE, Minneapolis, MN 55413
Telephone: 612-332-8344
Website: www.archantiques.com
E-mail: info@archantiques.com
All varieties of architectural artifacts, vintage lighting fixtures

Asia Minor Carpets

236 Fifth Ave., 2nd Floor, New York, NY 10001
Telephone: 212-447-9066 Fax: 212-447-1879
Website: www.asiaminorcarpets.com
Fine antique and newer Turkish carpets and kilims in traditional and Arts and Crafts designs

The Bath Works

4103 Old Hickory Blvd., Old Hickory, TN 37138
Telephone: 615-847-8621
Website: www.lustrebath.co.uk
Sales and renovation of antique bath tubs from America, England, and France

Bathroom Machineries

495 Main St., Murphys, CA 95247
Telephone: 209-728-2031 Fax: 209-728-2320
Website: www.deabath.com

Berman Gallery

9 Long Point Lane, Rose Valley, PA 19063
Telephone: 888-784-2554, 215-733-0707
Website: www.bermangallery.com
E-mail: BER441@aol.com
Mission furniture and Arts & Crafts accessories, also Stickley furniture

Circa 1910 Antiques

7206 Melrose Ave., Los Angeles, CA 90046
Telephone: 323-965-1910
Website: www.circa1910antiques.com
E-mail: west1910@pacbell.net
Authentic Arts and Crafts furniture, lighting, metalwork, pottery, accessories

City Lights Antique Lighting

2226 Massachusetts Avenue, Cambridge, MA 02140
Telephone: 617-547-1490 Fax: 617-479-2074
Website: www.citylights.nu
E-mail: lights@citylights.nu

Antique American and European light fixtures – many types and styles

Classic Ceramic tile

272 Hwy. 18 N, East Brunswick, NJ
Telephone: 732-390-7700 Fax: 732-390-6662
Website: www.classicceramictile.com
E-mail: tsoluri@eastcoasttile.com

Minton Hollins collection of period tile

DEA Bathroom Machineries

495 Main Street, Murphys, CA 95247
Telephone: 209-728-2031 Fax: 209-728-2320
Website: www.deabath.com

Antique and reproduction bathroom fixtures, fittings and accessories, many unusual items

Ed Donaldson Hardware Restoration

1488 North Road, Carlisle, PA 17013
Telephone: 717-249-3624 Fax: 717-249-5647
Website: www.eddonaldson.com
E-mail: ed@eddonaldson.com

Old and vintage hardware, restored antique hardware, new parts and pieces, antique locks

Eron Johnson Antiques, Ltd.

451 Broadway, Denver, CO 80203
Telephone: 303-777-8700 Fax: 303-777-8787
Website: www.antiques-internet.com
E-mail: eron@eronjohnsonantiques.com

Doors, fireplaces, capitals, fireplaces and accessories, stained glass, windows, iron doors/gates/arches/transoms, other architectural pieces

Eugenia's Antique hardware

5370 Peachtree Road, Chamblee, GA 30341
Telephone: 800-337-1677, 770-458-5966
Fax: 770-458-5966
Website: www.eugeniaantiquehardware.com
E-mail: eugeniashardware@mindspring.com

Door knockers, hinges, door plates, rosettes, twist bells, furniture and bathroom hardware

JMW Gallery

144 Lincoln St., Boston, MA 02111
Telephone: 617-338-9097 Fax: 617-338-7636
Website: www.jmwgallery.com
E-mail: mail@jmwgallery.com

Furniture, art pottery, woodblock prints - emphasis on Arts and Crafts period objects produced in New England

John Alexander Ltd.

10-12 W Gravers Ln., Philadelphia, PA 19118
Telephone: 215-242-0741
Website: www.johnalexander.com
E-mail: info@JohnAlexanderltd.com

Period Arts and Crafts furnishings and decorative arts in the British tradition

Just Art Pottery

6606 N. Rustic Oak Ct., Peoria, IL 61614
Telephone: 309-690-7966
Website: www.justartpottery.com
E-mail: gregmy@justartpottery.com

Antique American Art Pottery

Laguna

116 South Washington St., Seattle, WA 98104
Telephone: 206-682-6162
Website: www.lagunapottery.com/

Original Mission or Arts and Crafts era pottery, no reproductions

Legacy Building Supply

540 Division Street, Cobourg, ON
Telephone: 905-373-0796
Website: www.legacybs.com

Salvaged doors, windows, bathroom fixtures, plumbing, mantels, fireplace items, radiators, staircases, stained glass, hardware, bricks, beams and reclaimed lumber, flooring

Liz's Antique Hardware

453 S La Brea, Los Angeles, CA 90036
Telephone: 323-939-4403
Website: www.lahardware.com
E-mail: shop@lahardware.com

More than a million pieces of hardware (1850 to 1970) for doors, windows, cabinets, and furniture, contemporary and reproduction; also lighting and bath accessories

Londonderry Brasses Ltd.

PO Box 415, 736 Steelville Rd.,
Cochranville, PA 19330-0415
Telephone: 610-593-6239 Fax: 610-593-4788
Website: www.londonderry-brasses.com
E-mail: londonderry@epix.net

Large selection of fine brass furniture hardware, authentic reproduction hardware, and custom brass casting

LooLoo Design

255 Bristol Ferry Road, Portsmouth, RI 02871
Telephone: 800-508-0022
Website: www.looloodesign.com
E-mail: Jill@LooLooDesign.com

Antique plumbing fixtures and bath accessories

Luminaria Lighting

340 SE 6th Ave., Portland, OR 97210
Telephone: 800-638-5619 Fax: 831-423-0436
Website: www.luminarialighting.com
E-mail: customerservice@luminarialighting.com

Expertly restored antique light fixtures, custom reproductions, and original design work

Materials Unlimited

2 W Michigan Ave., Ypsilanti, MI 48197
Telephone: 800-299-9462 Fax: 734-482-3636
Website: www.materialsunlimited.com

Fine restored antique lighting, furniture, and architectural salvage

North Shore Architectural Antiques

521 7th St., Two Harbors, MN 55616
Telephone: 218-834-0018
Website: www.north-shore-architectural-antiques.com

Salvaged doors, windows, mantels, ceiling tin, lighting, electrical, plumbing and fixtures, tile, stone and pavers, columns, stairway components, more

Ohmega Salvage General Store

2400 San Pablo Ave., Berkeley, CA 94702
Telephone: 510-204-0767 Fax: 510-843-7123
Website: www.ohmegasalvage.com
E-mail: ohmegasalvage@earthlink.net

Salvaged doors, windows, mantels, lighting, cabinets, hardware, decorative elements

Old House Parts Company

24 Blue Wave Mall, Kennebunk, ME 04043
Telephone: 207-985-1999 Fax: 207-985-1911
Website: www.oldhouseparts.com
E-mail: parts@oldhouseparts.com

Antique doors, windows, lighting, mantles, plumbing fixtures, stairway parts, hardware, reclaimed wood, garden elements, and more. Restoration specialists, design services.

Omega Too

2204 San Pablo Ave., Berkeley, CA 94702
Telephone: 510-843-3636 Fax: 510-843-0666
Website: www.omegatoo.com
E-mail: megatoo@pacbell.net

Antique and reproduction lighting, bathroom fixtures and accessories, stained glass, Craftsman style doors, more

Randall Antiques and Fine Art

PO Box 357231, Gainesville, FL 32635-7231
Website: www.rafa.com

Extensive collection of art, ceramics and pottery, art glass, and items of the Arts and Crafts era

Re Use the Past

98 Moreland St., Grantville, GA 30220
Telephone: 770-583-3111
Website: www.reusethepast.com
E-mail: bocastle@mindspring.com

Heartpine flooring and doors, ceiling tin, doors, windows, stained glass, lighting, hardware, bricks and pavers

Rejuve Seattle

2910 1st Ave. S, Seattle, WA 98134
Telephone: 206-382-1901
Website: www.rejuvenation.com
E-mail: rejuveseattle@rejuvenation.com

Authentic period lighting; bath, cabinet, door and lighting hardware; hooks, brackets, coverplates, more

Rejuvenation

2550 NW Nicolai St., Portland, OR 97210
Telephone: 888-401-1900 Fax: 800-526-7329
Website: www.rejuvenation.com

Authentic period lighting; bath, cabinet, door and lighting hardware; hooks, brackets, coverplates, more

Restoration Resources

31 Thayer St., Boston, MA 02118
Telephone: 617-542-3033 Fax: 617-542-3034
Website: www.restorationresources.com (site being developed)

Extensive selection of antique hardware, fireplace mantels, leaded glass windows, plumbing fixtures, original lighting fixtures, hardwood doors, more

Robinson's Antiques

763 West Bippley Road, Lake Odessa, MI 48849
Telephone: 616-374-7750
Website: www.robinsonsantiques.com
E-mail: antiquehardware@robinsonsantiques.com

Extensive collection of antique hardware; mirror resilvering

Salvage Heaven, Inc.

206 E Lincoln Avenue, Milwaukee, WI 53207
Telephone: 414-482-0286 Fax: 414-482-0308
Website: www.salvageheaven.com
E-mail: recycle@SalvageHeaven.com

Doors, windows, lighting, electrical, tin ceiling, plumbing fixtures, fireplace components, flooring, moldings, wrought iron, bricks, pavers, more

Sylvan Brandt

651 E Main St., Lititz, PA 17543
Telephone: 717-626-4520
Website: www.sylvanbrandt.com

Antique and resawn salvaged flooring; also reclaimed old doors, windows, architectural elements, and hardware

Timeless Classic Elegance

3035 Barat Road, Montreal, Quebec, CA, H3Y 2H6
Telephone: 514-935-5196
Website: www.trocadero.com
E-mail: eserafini@timelessclassicelegance.com

Antique leaded stained glass windows from the UK

Van Dyke's Restorers

PO Box 278, 39771 SD Hwy. 34,
Woonsocket, SD 57385
Telephone: 800-787-3355
Website: www.vandykes.com

All types of period hardware, woodwork, furniture, accessories

Voorhees Craftsman

1415 N Lake Ave., Pasadena, CA 91104
Telephone: 888-982-6377
Website: www.voorheescraftsman.com
E-mail: steve@voorheescraftsman.com

Fine Arts & Crafts antique furniture, plus quality reproductions

RESTORATION/REPRODUCTION SUPPLIERS

Advanced Refinishing

Rochelle, IL 61068
Telephone: 877-562-8468
Website: www.advancedrefinishing.com
E-mail: sales@advancedrefinishing.com

Specializing in claw foot and pedestal tubs, reproduction plumbing fixtures, everything for antique bathrooms, restore all types of bathtubs.

Affordable Antique Bath & More

4829 Dalewood Dr., El Dorado Hills, CA 95762
Telephone: 888-303-2284, 916-941-6460
Fax: 916-941-6470
Website: www.bathandmore.com
E-mail: sales@bathandmore.com

Antique and reproduction plumbing fixtures, bathroom hardware and accessories

American Bath Factory

13395 Estelle St., Corona, CA 92879
Telephone: 800-454-2284
Website: www.americanbathfactory.com
E-mail: info@americanbathfactory.com

Victorian tub faucets with matching lavatory and accessories, claw-foot whirlpool and air-jet bathtubs

Black Cove Cabinetry

137 Pleasant Hill Rd., Scarborough, ME 04074
Telephone: 800-262-8979
Website: www.blackcove.com

Custom kitchen cabinetry in many period styles; soapstone, slate, and granite kitchen counters

Clawfoot Supply

Off I-275, Erlanger, KY
Telephone: 877-682-4192
Website: www.clawfootsupply.com
E-mail: sales@clawfootsupply.com

Historic and reproduction fixtures for period bath restoration

DEA Bathroom Machineries

495 Main Street, Murphys, CA 95247
Telephone: 209-728-2031 Fax: 209-728-2320
Website: www.deabath.com

Antique and reproduction bathroom fixtures, fittings and accessories, many unusual items

Del Mondo

PO Box 488, 116 Boston Rd., Groton, MA 01450
Telephone: 978-449-0091
Website: www.delmondolp.com
E-mail: info@delmondolp.com

Period European bathroom, tile and stone products

Elkay Manufacturing Company

2222 Camden Ct., Oak Brook, IL 60523
Telephone: 630-574-8484 Fax: 630-574-5012
Website: www.elkayusa.com

Specialty collection sinks in a variety of metals and finishes, luxury faucet products and accessories

Ginger

460-N Greenway Industrial Dr.,
Fort Mill, SC 29708-8117
Telephone: 888-469-6511
Website: www.gingerco.com
E-mail: info@gingerco.com (sister brand of Motiv)

Fine bathroom accessories, lighting, and decorative hardware

Good Time Stove Co.

PO Box 306, Rte. 112, Goshen, MA 01032
Telephone: 888-282-7506, 413-268-3677
Website: www.goodtimestove.com
E-mail: stoveprincess@goodtimestove.com

Authentic antique kitchen ranges and heating stoves, fully restored and functional: enamel, cast iron, wood, wood-gas combos, conversions available

Grohe America

241 Covington Dr., Bloomingsdale, IL 60108
Telephone: 630-582-7711 Fax: 630-582-7722
Website: www.groheamerica.com

German-engineered kitchen and bath faucets and shower products

Harrington Brass Works

7 Pearl Ct., Allendale, NJ 07401
Telephone: 201-818-1300
Website: www.harringtonbrassworks.com

Victorian, classic, and contemporary faucets and bathroom accessories

Heartland Appliances

1050 Fountain St., Cambridge, ON N3H 4R7 Canada
Telephone: 519-650-5501 Fax: 519-650-3773
Website: www.heartlandappliances.com

Modern amenities in a classic range style; ovens and refrigerators also

Kolson

653 Middle Neck Rd., Great Neck, NY 11023
Telephone: 516-487-1224 Fax: 516-487-1231
Website: www.kolson.com
E-mail: kolsongn@optonline.net

Door and cabinet hardware, faucets, sinks, tubs, toilets, mirrors, medicine cabinets, bathroom accessories

Lefroy Brooks

16 Crosby St., New York, NY 10013
Telephone: 212-226-2242 Fax: 212-226-3003
Website: www.lefroybrooks.com
E-mail: lbinfo@lefroybrooks.com

Wide selection of English-manufactured bathroom fixtures, all tooled for the American Market

Mac the Antique Plumber

6325 Elvas Ave., Sacramento, CA 95819
Telephone: 800-916-2284
Website: www.antiqueplumber.com
Visually authentic antique plumbing fixtures with modern mechanicals, hardware

Omega Too

2204 San Pablo Ave., Berkeley, CA 94702
Telephone: 510-843-3636 Fax: 510-843-0666
Website: www.omegatoo.com
E-mail: megatoo@pacbell.net
Antique and reproduction lighting, bathroom fixtures and accessories, stained glass, Craftsman style doors, more

Renovator's Supply

Renovator's Old Mill, Millers Falls, MA 01349
Telephone: 800-659-2211
Website: www.rensup.com
Restoration plumbing, hardware, and lighting; bathroom fixtures and accessories

Sunrise Specialty Co.

930 98th Ave., Oakland, CA 94603-2306
Telephone: 510-729-7277 Fax: 510-729-7270
Website: www.sunrisespecialty.com
Full line of antique-style bathroom fixtures and fittings, kitchen faucets

Cobre / Susan Hebert Imports

1231 NW Hoyt St., Space #B-5, Portland, OR 97209
Telephone: 503-248-1111
Website: www.ecobre.com
Decorative and hand-crafted copper sinks and accessories

Urban Archaeology

143 Franklin St., New York, NY 10013
Telephone: 212-431-4646
Custom historically accurate console sinks, washstands, medicine cabinets, vanities; plus tile, mosaic, and stone

Wellborn Cabinetry

PO Box 1210, Ashland, AL 36251
Telephone: 800-336-8040 Fax: 256-354-7022
Website: www.wellborn.com
Semi-custom fine kitchen and bath cabinetry

Wentworth Furniture Company

1910 NW 18th St., Pompano Beach, FL 33069
Telephone: 954-973-8312
Website: www.wentworthfurniture.com
Fine handmade custom kitchen furniture, period finishing

Vintage Plumbing Bathroom Antiques

Website sales only
9645 Sylvia Ave., Northridge, CA 91324
Telephone: 818-772-1721
Website: www.vintageplumbing.com
Victorian, Arts & Crafts, and Art Deco bathroom fixtures and fittings – no reproductions

Vintage Tub and Bath

534 W Green St., Hazleton, PA 18201
Telephone: 877-868-1369, 570-450-7925
Fax: 570-450-7926
Website: www.vintagetub.com
E-mail: supply@vintagetub.com
Many styles of new and vintage tubs, faucets and fittings, vanities, bathroom mirrors, more

Willow Glen Kitchen & Bath

351 Willow St., San Jose, CA 95110
Telephone: 408-293-2284
Website: www.willowglen.com
Reproduction Arts and Crafts lighting, cabinets

PLUMBING

A-Ball Plumbing Supply

1703 W Burnside St., Portland, OR 97209
Telephone: 800-228-0134 Fax: 503-228-0030
Website: www.a-ball.com
Traditional plumbing fixtures, floor grates, switch plates and outlet covers

Advanced Refinishing

Rochelle, IL 61068
Telephone: 877-562-8468
Website: www.advancedrefinishing.com
E-mail: sales@advancedrefinishing.com
Specializing in claw foot and pedestal tubs, reproduction plumbing fixtures, everything for antique bathrooms, restore all types of bathtubs.

Affordable Antique Bath & More

4829 Dalewood Dr., El Dorado Hills, CA 95762
Telephone: 888-303-2284, 916-941-6460
Fax: 916-941-6470
Website: www.bathandmore.com
E-mail: sales@bathandmore.com
Antique & reproduction plumbing fixtures, bathroom hardware &accessories

American Bath Factory

13395 Estelle St., Corona, CA 92879
Telephone: 800-454-2284
Website: www.americanbathfactory.com
E-mail: info@americanbathfactory.com
Victorian tub faucets with matching lavatory and accessories, clawfoot whirlpool and air-jet bathtubs

Antique Hardware and Home

39771 SD Hwy. 34, PO Box 278,
Woonsocket, SD 57385
Telephone: 877-823-7567
Website: www.antiquehardware.com
Faucets and bath accessories, door and cabinet hardware, tin ceilings, appliances, lights, shades, more

Antique Sink

PO Box 26, 506 Cassin Ave., Newell, PA 15466
Telephone: 877-800-4100, 724-938-9727
Website: www.antiquesink.com
E-mail: mail@antiquesink.com
Custom copper or ceramic sinks, antique-style faucets, hand-crafted antique-styled vanities

Architectural Detail

299 N Altadena Dr., Pasadena, CA 91107
Telephone: 626-844-6670 Fax: 626-844-6651
Website: www.pasadenasalvage.com
Vintage plumbing fixtures and fittings

Harrington Brass Works

7 Pearl Ct., Allendale, NJ 07401
Telephone: 201-818-1300
Website: www.harringtonbrassworks.com
Victorian, classic, and contemporary faucets and bathroom accessories

Kolson

653 Middle Neck Rd., Great Neck, NY 11023
Telephone: 516-487-1224 Fax: 516-487-1231
Website: www.kolson.com
E-mail: kolsongn@optonline.net
Door and cabinet hardware, faucets, sinks, tubs, toilets, mirrors, medicine cabinets, bathroom accessories

Lefroy Brooks

16 Crosby St., New York, NY 10013
Telephone: 212-226-2242 Fax: 212-226-3003
Website: www.lefroybrooks.com
E-mail: lbinfo@lefroybrooks.com
Wide selection of English-manufactured bathroom fixtures, all tooled for the American Market

Mac the Antique Plumber

6325 Elvas Ave., Sacramento, CA 95819
Telephone: 800-916-2284
Website: www.antiqueplumber.com
Visually authentic antique plumbing fixtures with modern mechanicals, hardware

Renovator's Supply

Renovator's Old Mill, Millers Falls, MA 01349
Telephone: 800-659-2211
Website: www.rensup.com
Restoration plumbing, hardware, and lighting; bathroom fixtures and accessories

Salvage Heaven, Inc.

206 E Lincoln Avenue, Milwaukee, WI 53207
Telephone: 414-482-0286 Fax: 414-482-0308
Website: www.salvageheaven.com
E-mail: recycle@SalvageHeaven.com
Doors, windows, lighting, electrical, tin ceiling, plumbing fixtures, fireplace components, flooring, moldings, wrought iron, bricks, pavers, more

Sunrise Specialty Co.

930 98th Ave., Oakland, CA 94603-2306
Telephone: 510-729-7277 Fax: 510-729-7270
Website: www.sunrisespecialty.com

Full line of antique-style bathroom fixtures and fittings, kitchen faucets

Vintage Plumbing Bathroom Antiques

Website sales only
9645 Sylvia Ave., Northridge, CA 91324
Telephone: 818-772-1721
Website: www.vintageplumbing.com

Victorian, Arts & Crafts, and Art Deco bathroom fixtures and fittings – no reproductions

Vintage Tub and Bath

534 W Green St., Hazleton, PA 18201
Telephone: 877-868-1369, 570-450-7925
Fax: 570-450-7926
Website: www.vintagetub.com
E-mail: supply@vintagetub.com

Many styles of new and vintage tubs, faucets and fittings, vanities, bathroom mirrors, more

FURNITURE AND CABINETS

American Furnishings

1409 W Third Ave., Columbus, OH 43212,
2 other locations
Telephone: 614-488-7263
Website: www.americanfurnishings.com
E-mail: info@americanfurnishings.com

Hand-crafted furniture, lighting, glasswork, pottery, and accessories

Arnold d'Epagnier

14201 Notley Road, Colesville, MD 20904
Telephone: 301-384-3201
Website: www.missionevolution.com
E-mail: info@missionevolution.com

Custom furniture pieces in the style of Greene and Greene

Art Furniture

158 Camden St., London NW1 9PA
Telephone: +44 0044 207 267 4324
Website: www.artfurniture.co.uk
E-mail: arts-and-crafts@artfurniture.co.uk

Extensive collection, works by Liberty & Co., Shapland & Petter, Heals, Wylie, Lochead, Baillie-Scott, E.A. Taylor, George Walton, more

Arts and Crafts Antiques

Manchester, Northwest UK
Telephone: +44 0161 945 7775
Website: www.artsandcraftsantiques.com
E-mail: David@artsandcraftsantiques.com

Specializing in golden oak furniture, other items also stocked

Arts & Crafts Industries

6400 Variel Ave., Woodland Hills, CA 91367-2577
Telephone: 818-610-0490

Heirloom-quality Arts & Crafts furniture

Berkeley Mills East-West Furniture Design

2830 7th St., Berkeley, CA 94710
Telephone: 510-549-2854 Fax: 510-548-0865
Website: www.berkeleymills.com
E-mail: shop@berkeleymills.com

Custom-made furniture in a wide range of styles and woods

Berman Gallery

9 Long Point Lane, Rose Valley, PA 19063
Telephone: 888-784-2554, 215-733-0707
Website: www.bermangallery.com
E-mail: BER441@aol.com

Mission furniture and Arts & Crafts accessories, also Stickley furniture

Birdseye Building Company

3104 Huntington Rd., Richmond, VT 05477
Telephone: 802-434-2112 Fax: 802-434-3540
Website: www.birdseyebuilding.com
E-mail: info@birdseyebuilding.com

Hand-crafted, custom-designed vanities, furniture, built-ins, and entry doors in an assortment of traditional and contemporary styles; also metal and glass work

Black Cove Cabinetry

137 Pleasant Hill Rd., Scarborough, ME 04074
Telephone: 800-262-8979
Website: www.blackcove.com

Custom kitchen cabinetry in many period styles; soapstone, slate, and granite kitchen counters

Black River Mission

PO Box 146, Milford, NY 13807
Telephone: 607-286-7641
Website: www.blackrivermission.com

Hand-crafted, hand-finished Arts & Crafts and Mission-Style furniture

C. H. Becksvoort

PO Box 12, New Gloucester, ME 04260
Telephone: 207-926-4608
Website: www.chbecksvoort.com

Artisan-made Shaker-inspired and reproduction furniture

Charles L. Nazarian Designer

956 Washington St., Gloucester, MA 01930
Telephone: 978-281-4448 Fax: 978-281-8569

Architectural woodworking, lighting, liturgical interiors and furnishings

Circa 1910 Antiques

7206 Melrose Ave., Los Angeles, CA 90046
Telephone: 323-965-1910
Website: www.circa1910antiques.com
E-mail: west1910@pacbell.net

Authentic Arts and Crafts furniture, lighting, metalwork, pottery, accessories

Coppa Woodworking

1231 Paraiso Ave., San Pedro, CA 90731
Telephone: 310-548-5332 Fax: 310-548-6740
Website: www.coppawoodworking.com

Custom woodworking and Adirondack furniture

The County Seat

Huntercombe Manor Barn, Nr Henley on Thames, Oxon RG9 5RY UK
Telephone: +44 1491 641349 Fax: +44 1491 641533
Website: www.thecountyseat.com

Architect designed furniture from the 19th and 20th centuries, related Art pottery, metalwork and glass

Crafts Nouveau

112 Alexandra Park Road, Muswell Hill,
London N10 2AE
Telephone: +44 0 20 8444 3300
Website: www.craftsnouveau.co.uk
E-mail: lauriestrange@msn.com

Quality furniture and decorative items of the Arts and Crafts and Art Nouveau periods

Crown Point Cabinetry

153 Charlestown Rd., Claremont, NH 03743
Telephone: 800-999-4994 Fax: 800-370-1218
Website: www.crown-point.com

Handcrafted, period styling custom cabinetry

Darrell Peart Furnituremaker

3419 C St. NE, #16, Auburn, WA 98002
Telephone: 425-277-4070
Website: www.furnituremaker.com

Custom-made furniture in the styles of Greene & Greene

Debey Zito Fine Furniture Making

PO Box 881841, San Francisco, CA 94188
Telephone: 415-922-7444

Artisan guild member - Custom and limited production furniture

Falcon Designs

PO Box 50065, Eugene, Or 97405
Telephone: 541-937-3060
Website: www.falcon-designs.com
E-mail: info@falcon-designs.com

Heirloom-quality furniture in Shaker, Mission, Arts & Crafts, and Asian designs

Floating Stone Woodworks

88 Hatch St. #406, New Bedford, MA 02746
Telephone: 800-267-1079, 508-997-1079
Website: www.floatingstonewoodworks.com

Hand-crafted custom wood furniture in styles influenced by designs of Gustav Stickley and Greene & Greene

H. L. Ranch

114 E Lemon Ave., Monrovia, CA 91016
Telephone: 626-303-4899 Fax: 626-358-6159
Website: www. hlranch.com
E-mail: sales@historiclighting.com

Arts and Crafts furniture, lighting, and decorative accessories

Harvest House

1 Proctor Rd., Schomberg, ON L0G 1T0 Canada
Telephone: 888-241-9960 (in Canada);
877-939-8606 (in USA)
160 King St. E, Toronto, ON M5A 1J3
Telephone: 866-852-1306, 416-862-9449
Website: www.harvesthouse.on.ca
E-mail: info@harvesthouse.on.ca
*Hand-made, solid wood furniture, emphasis on Mission
styling*

Helmstown

218 S Brindlee Mtn. Parkway, Arab, AL 35016
Telephone: 888-VANITURE; 256-586-0951
Website: www.helmstown.com
E-mail: helmstown@earthlink.net
*Custom antique-styled furniture: vanities, wall mirrors,
linen cabinets, kitchen cupboards, buffets, worktables, more*

Historic Lighting

114 E Lemon Ave., Monrovia, CA 91016
Telephone: 626-303-4899
Website: www.HistoricLighting.com
*Mission furniture, art pottery, hand-crafted carpets,
period lighting and accessories; custom work*

JMW Gallery

144 Lincoln St., Boston, MA 02111
Telephone: 617-338-9097 Fax: 617-338-7636
Website: www.jmwgallery.com
E-mail: mail@jmwgallery.com
*Furniture, art pottery, woodblock prints - emphasis on
Arts and Crafts period objects produced in New England*

John Alexander Ltd.

10-12 W Gravers Ln., Philadelphia, PA 19118
Telephone: 215-242-0741
Website: www.johnalexander.com
E-mail: info@JohnAlexanderltd.com
*Period Arts and Crafts furnishings and decorative arts in
the British tradition*

Kennebeck Company

1 Front St., Bath, ME 04530
Telephone: 207-443-2131
Website: www.kennebeccompany.com
E-mail: info@.kennebeccompany.com
Custom cabinetry in many period styles

L. & J. G. Stickley

PO Box 480, 1 Stickley Dr., Manlius, NY 13104-0480
Telephone: 315-682-5500 Fax: 315-682-6306
Website: www.stickley.com
*Reissues of original Stickley furniture designs in a variety of
collection lines, upholstered furniture, rugs, decorative acces-
sories. No direct sales, through distributors only.*

Lutyens Design Associates

3 Edgerton Terrace, London, SW3 2BX
Telephone: +44 207-589-2347 Fax: +44 838-1030
Website: www.lutyens-furniture.com
E-mail: info@lutyens-furniture.com
Furniture, lighting, and designs in the style of Sir Edwin Lutyens

Mack & Rodel Cabinetmakers

44 Leighton Rd., Pownal, ME 04069
Telephone: 207-688-4483
E-mail: macrodel@aol.com
*Original furniture designs influenced by major Arts & Crafts
designers*

Mark Golding

25A Clifton Terrace, Brighton, Sussex BN1 3HA
Telephone: +44 0 1273 327774 / +44 0 7775 535453
Website: www.achome.co.uk
E-mail: mark@achome.co.uk
*Morris wallpapers and fabrics, items by Voysey, Dresser,
Godwin, Pugin, de Morgan, more*

Merillat Industries

Website: www.merillat.com
*Premier cabinetry in a multitude of styles, finishes, moldings,
and hardware; sold through local dealers only*

Michael Fitzsimmons Decorative Arts

311 W Superior Street, Chicago, Il 60610
Telephone: 312-787-0496 Fax: 312-787-6343
Website: www.fitzdecarts.com
E-mail: mfda311@ameritech.net
*Full range of period reproduction furniture plus selected
antiques (furniture, lighting, metalware, ceramics, textiles)*

**Mitchell Andrus Studios
(Roycroft Renaissance Artisan)**

68 Central Ave., Stirling, NJ 07980
Telephone: 908-647-7442 Fax: 908-647-4090
Website: www.mitchellandrus.com
*Furniture and accessories in authentic arts and Crafts styles,
custom framing als*

N. R. Hiller Design

908 S Rogers St., Bloomington, IN 47403
Telephone: 812-825-5872
Website: www.nrhiller@bloomington.in.us
Custom-designed cabinets and furniture

New West

2811 Big Horn Ave., Cody, WY 82414
Telephone: 800-653-2391
Website: www.newest.com
*Fusion of Arts and Crafts and "Cowboy Style"—
furniture, lighting, accessories*

Old Ways Ltd.

39 Barton Ave. SE, Minneapolis, MN 55414
Telephone: 612-379-2142
Website: www.oldwaysltd.com
Hand-crafted tabletop furniture, housewares, textiles, endpapers

Paul Downs Cabinetmakers

401 E 4th St., Building 8, 4th floor,
Bridgeport, PA 19405
Telephone: 610-664-9902 Fax: 610-664-9997
Website: www.pauldowns.com
E-mail: pauldowns@pauldowns.com
*Tables, chairs, servers, bedroom, dining room, office furniture
and bookcases*

Paul Reeves

32B Kensington Church Street, London W8 4HA UK
Telephone: +44 0 207 937 1594
Fax: +44 0 207 938 2163
Website: www.paulreeveslondon.com
*Comprehensive selection of Arts and Crafts antiques, also loan to
museums*

Pendleton Woodworks

2631 Island Hwy. West, Qualicum Beach,
BC V9K 1G7, Canada
Telephone: 250-752-1184
Website: www.pendletonwoodworks.com
*Arts and Crafts-style stained glass lamps, furniture, accessories,
fabrics*

Plain and Fancy Custom Cabinetry

Route 51 & Oak St., Schaefferstown, PA 17088
Telephone: 800-447-9006
Website: www.plainfancy.com
Custom cabinetry in many period styles; dealers nationwide

Present Time

18452 Skagit City Rd., Mount Vernon, WA 98273
Telephone: 360-445-4702
Website: www.present-time-clocks.com
E-mail: jim@present-time-clocks.com
Hand-made clocks in the Craftsman style

Puritan Values at the Dome

The Dome, St. Edmunds Rd.,
Southwold, Suffolk IP18 6BZ
Telephone: +44 0 1502 722211
69 Kensington Church St., London W8 4BG
Telephone: +44 0 207 937 2410
Website: www.puritanvalues.co.uk
E-mail: Sales@puritanvalues.com

Quality Custom Cabinetry (Affiliated Dealers)

PO Box 189, 125 Peters Rd., New Holland, PA 17557
Telephone: 800-909-6006
Website: www.qcc.com
Custom cabinetry in many period styles; dealers nationwide

Remains To Be Seen

62 Wyle Cop, Shrewsbury, Shropshire SY1 1UX
Telephone: +44 0 1743 361560
Website: www.remainstobeseen.co.uk
E-mail: noovo@tiscali.co.uk
*(Affiliated Dealers) Quality furniture and decorative items of
the Arts and Crafts and Art Nouveau periods*

Roycroft Copper

Manhattan, NY 10001-1538
E-mail: bigfatty@roycroftcopper.com
Small Roycroft-style furniture and accessories

Sawbridge Studios

153 W Ohio St., Chicago, IL 60610
Telephone: 312-828-0055
Website: www.sawbridge.com
Hand-crafted furniture and accessories

Sligh Furniture Company

1201 Industrial Ave., Holland, MI 49423
Telephone: 616-392-7101
Website: www.sligh.com
E-mail: rob@sligh.com

Fine furniture, clocks

Strachan Antiques

40, Darnley St., Pollokshields,
Glasgow, G41 2Se Scotland
Telephone: +44 0 141 429 4411
Website: www.strachanantiques.co.uk.com

Comprehensive selection of Arts and Crafts furniture

Strictly Wood

4501 Greenpoint Dr., Ste. 106,
Greensboro, NC 27410
Telephone: 800-278-2019 Fax: 336-931-6201
Website: www.StrictlyWoodFurniture.com
E-mail: info@StrictlyWoodFurniture.com

Hand-crafted, solid wood furniture in period styles

Thomas Strangeland Artist/Craftsman

312 S Lucille St., Seattle, WA 98108
Telephone: 206-622-2004
Website: www.artistcraftsman.net
E-mail: info@artistcraftsman.net

Custom-designed, fine wood furniture in the style of Greene and Greene

Thos. Moser Cabinetmakers

149 Main St., Freeport, ME 04032
Telephone: 800-862-1973
Website: www.thosmoser.com
E-mail: service@thosmoser.com

Showrooms in New York, Chicago, San Francisco, Seattle, Boston, DC, Columbus, OH, and Freeport, ME. Fine furniture in Shaker, Arts & Crafts, and other 19th century furniture forms

Trustworth Studios

PO Box 1109, Plymouth, MA 02362
Telephone: 508-746-1847 Fax: 508-746-3736
Website: www.trustworth.com
E-mail: voyseyboy@trustworth.com

Custom period lighting, wallpaper, clocks, furniture; needlework and accessories in the Voysey line

Warren Hile Studio

1823 Enterprise Way, Monrovia, CA 91016

Full line of hand-crafted Mission furniture

Wellborn Cabinetry

PO Box 1210, Ashland, AL 36251
Telephone: 800-336-8040 Fax: 256-354-7022
Website: www.wellborn.com

Semi-custom fine kitchen and bath cabinetry

Wentworth Furniture Company

1910 NW 18th St., Pompano Beach, FL 33069
Telephone: 954-973-8312
Website: www.wentworthfurniture.com

Fine handmade custom kitchen furniture, period finishing

Whit McLeod

PO Box 132, Arcata, CA 95518
Telephone: 707-822-7307
Website: www.whitmcleod.com
E-mail: info@whitmcleod.com

Arts and Crafts style furniture from reclaimed and salvaged materials

Willow Glen Kitchen & Bath

351 Willow St., San Jose, CA 95110
Telephone: 408-293-2284
Website: www.willowglen.com

Reproduction Arts and Crafts lighting, cabinets

Wood Essentials

PO Box 843, Lenox Hill Station,
New York, NY 10021
Telephone: 212-717-1112 Fax: 212-717-5235
Website: www.woodessentials.com

Hand-crafted medicine cabinets in traditional styles, finished or unfinished, four hardwood choices

Yester Year's Vintage Doors & Millwork

66 S. Main St., Hammond, NY 13646
Telephone: 800-787-2001, 315-324-5250
Fax: 315-324-6531
Website: www.vintagedoors.com

Solid wood vintage door manufacturer featuring screen/storm doors, interior and exterior entrance doors, louver, French, and Dutch doors

CERAMICS, TILE, GLASS, POTTERY

AD Antiques

PO Box 2407, Stone, Staffordshire ST15 8WY
Telephone: +44 0 7811 783518
Website: www.adantiques.com

Pottery and ceramics, metalwork, other decorative arts

American Furnishings

1409 W Third Ave., Columbus, OH 43212,
2 other locations
Telephone: 614-488-7263
Website: www.americanfurnishings.com
E-mail: info@americanfurnishings.com

Hand-crafted furniture, lighting, glasswork, pottery, and accessories

American Restoration Tile

11416 Otter Creek S Rd., Mabelvale, AR 72103
Telephone: 501-570-0300 Fax: 501-455-1004
Website: www.reswtorationtile.com
E-mail: bebyrd@reswtorationtile.com

Custom tiles to match old patterns and sizes

Antique Articles

PO Box 72, Dunstable, MA 01827
Telephone: 978-649-4983
Website: www.antiquearticles.com
E-mail: articles@antiquearticles.com

Guaranteed original European and American ceramic tiles, mostly from 1650-1930's

Architectural Ceramic Products

631 Boardman-Canfield Rd., Boardman, OH 44512
Telephone: 330-758-0835

Ceramic and art tiles, custom murals, ceramic roof tiles, salvaged architectural building products

Artisan Sonoma Pottery

575 Solano Ave., Sonoma, CA 95476
Telephone: 707-996-2192
Website: www.artisanknobs.com

Hand-thrown pottery and porcelain door and cabinet hardware in the Arts and Crafts style

Bendheim

61 Willett St., Passaic, NJ 07055
Telephone: 800-221-7379
Showroom: 122 Hudson St., New York, NY 10013
Telephone: 212-226-6370

*West coast: Oakland, CA; telephone: 800-900-3499
Website: www.originalrestorationglass.com
Importer of mouth-blown and UV Restoration‰ glass for period houses*

Blenko Glass

PO Box 67, Milton, WV 25541
Telephone: 304-743-9081
Website: www.blenkoglass.com

Mouth-blown sheet and slab glass, stained glass, blanks for etching

Carreaux Du Nord

2501 Washington St., Two Rivers, WI 54241
Telephone: 920-553-5303
Website: www.carreauxdunord.com

Hand-made art tiles in historic and Arts and Crafts motifs, also wrought iron, and Arts and Crafts mantle clocks

Charles Rupert Designs

2005 Oak Bay Ave., Victoria, BC V8R 1E5, Canada
Telephone: 250-592-4916
Website: www.charles-rupert.com

Reproduction wallpaper, fabrics, art tile, and home accessories in a number of styles

Dard Hunter Studios (Roycroft)

Mountain House, 8 Highland Ave., PO Box 771,
Chillicothe, OH 45601
Telephone: 740-774-1236 Fax: 740-779-3273
Website: www.dardhunter.com
E-mail: info@dardhunter.com

*Pottery, frames, paper and prints, jewelry, more; maintained
by the grandson of Dard Hunter*

Del Mondo

PO Box 488, 116 Boston Rd., Groton, MA 01450
Telephone: 978-449-0091
Website: www.delmondolp.com
E-mail: info@delmondolp.com

Period European bathroom, tile and stone product

Derby Pottery and Tile

2029 Magazine St., New Orleans, LA 70130
Telephone: 504-586-9003
Website: www.derbypottery.com
E-mail: info@derbypottery.com

*Hand-pressed and finished reproduction tile for fireplaces,
backsplashes, tubs and shower surrounds*

Designs in Tile

PO Box 358, Mt. Shasta, CA 96067
Telephone: 530-926-2629 Fax: 530-926-6467
Website: www.designsintile.com
E-mail: info@designsintile.com

*All custom work, no stock - Period tiles and murals, subway
tile, molded trim, historic mosaic flooring*

Door Pottery

PO Box 14557, Madison, WI 53714
Telephone: 608-240-1626 Fax: 608-240-1626
Website: www.doorpottery.com
E-mail: sales@doorpottery.com

Hand-crafted vases in the Arts & Crafts style, garden pottery

Duquella Tile & Clayworks

PO Box 90065, Portland, OR 97290-0065
Telephone: 866-218-8221, 503-256-8330
Website: www.tiledecorative.com

*Hand-crafted, custom tile for kitchens, baths, and fireplaces;
custom work*

Ephraim Faience Pottery

PO Box 168, Deerfield, WI 53531
Telephone: 888-704-POTS Fax: 608-764-8439
Website: www.ephraimpottery.com
E-mail: sales@ephraimpottery.com

Hand-crafted art pottery and tile in the Arts & Crafts style

Fair Oak Workshops (artisan collective)

PO Box 5578, River Forest, IL 60305
Telephone: 800-341-0597 Fax: 708-366-3876
Website: www.fairoak.com

*Reproduction lighting, metalware, pottery, textiles, stencils,
jewelry and accessories*

Glasgow Style

Glasgow, Scotland
Website: www.glasgow-style.co.uk
E-mail: enquiries@glasgow-style.co.uk

*Specialize in Scottish pottery and Glasgow Girls ceramics,
large selection of other items*

Hill House Antiques & Decorative Arts

PO Box 17320, 18 Chelsea Manor Street,
London SW3 2WR UK
Telephone: +44 0 7973 842777
Website: www.hillhouse-antiques.co.uk

*Metalware, ceramics, small furniture, pictures and prints,
more*

Jeffrey Court

369 Meyer Circle, Corona, CA 92879
Telephone: 909-340-3383
Website: www.jeffreycourt.com

*Hand-crafted, hand-painted relief tile in many shapes,
styles, forms, and glazes*

JMW Gallery

144 Lincoln St., Boston, MA 02111
Telephone: 617-338-9097
Fax: 617-338-7636
Website: www.jmwgallery.com
E-mail: mail@jmwgallery.com

*Furniture, art pottery, woodblock prints - emphasis on Arts
and Crafts period objects produced in New England*

John Alexander Ltd.

10-12 W Gravers Ln., Philadelphia, PA 19118
Telephone: 215-242-0741
Website: www.johnalexander.com
E-mail: info@JohnAlexanderltd.com

*Period Arts and Crafts furnishings and decorative arts
in the British traditi*

Just Art Pottery

6606 N. Rustic Oak Ct., Peoria, IL 61614
Telephone: 309-690-7966
Website: www.justartpottery.com
E-mail: gregmy@justartpottery.com

Antique American Art Pottery

Katrich Studios

301 N Military, Dearborn, MI 48124
Telephone: 313-359-3400
Website: www.katrich.com
E-mail: luster@katrich.com

Unique, hand-thrown lusterware art pottery

L'Esperance Tile

237 Sheridan Ave., Albany, NY 12210
Telephone: 518-884-2814 Fax: 518-465-5586`

*Custom-made encaustic, geometric, mosaic, and
other traditional ceramic tiles*

Laguna

116 South Washington St., Seattle, WA 98104
Telephone: 206-682-6162
Website: www.lagunapottery.com/

Original Mission or Arts and Crafts era pottery, no reproductions

Lundberg Studios

PO Box C, 131 Old Coast Rd., Davenport, CA 95017
Telephone: 888-423-9711, 831-423-2532
FAX: 831-423-0436
Website: www.lundbergstudios.com

Lighting, lamps, vases, bottles, custom work

Mark Golding

25A Clifton Terrace, Brighton, Sussex BN1 3HA
Telephone: +44 0 1273 327774 / +44 0 7775 535453
Website: www.achome.co.uk
E-mail: mark@achome.co.uk

*Morris wallpapers and fabrics, items by Voysey, Dresser,
Godwin, Pugin, de Morgan, more*

Meredith Collection/Ironrock capital

PO Box 8854, Canton, OH 44711
Telephone: 330-484-1656 Fax: 330-484-9380
Website: www.meredithtile.com

*Hand-crafted and painted Victorian and Arts and Crafts tile
designs, moldings, liners, and field tile; many glazes and finishes available*

Mission Tile West

853 Mission St., South Pasadena, CA 91030
Telephone: 626-799-4595 Fax: 626-799-8769
Website: www.missiontilewest.com
E-mail: southpasadena@missiontilewest.com

Fine reproduction art tile in the Arts and Crafts style

Moravian Pottery and Tile Works

130 Swamp Rd., Doylestown, PA 18901
Telephone: 215-345-6722
Website: mptw.go.to.moravianpotteryandtileworks
@co.bucks.pa.us

Reproductions of the tile designs of Henry Chapman Mercer

Motawi Tileworks

170 Enterprise Dr., Ann Arbor, MI 48103
Telephone: 734-213-0017 Fax: 734-213-2569
Website: www.motawi.com

*Hand-made tiles in many Arts and Crafts and Art Nouveau
designs, plus historical motifs; matte finishes and crackle glazes*

Original Style Ltd.

Falcon Road, Sowton Industrial Estate,
Exter, EX2 7LF, UK
Telephone: (11) 44-1392-473-000
Fax: (11) 44-1392-473-003
Website: www.originalstyle.com
E-mail: info@originalstyle.com

Paint, stone, glass mosaic tiles, ceramic wall and floor tiles

Pairpoint Glassworks

PO Box 515, Sagamore, MA 02561
Telephone: 800-899-0953 Fax: 508-888-3537
Website: www.pairpoint.com
Hand-blown vases, stemware, decanters, and other accessories

Pewabic Pottery

10125 E Jefferson Ave., Detroit, MI 48214
Telephone: 313-822-0954 Fax: 313-822-6266
Website: www.pewabic.com
E-mail: pewabic1.pewabic.com
Arts and Crafts art tile and art pottery

Pratt & Larson Ceramics

1201 SE Third St., Portland, OR 97214
Telephone: 503-231-9464
Website: www.prattandlarson.com
*Hand-crafted tile in multiple styles, colors, and glazes;
sales through dealers only*

Randall Antiques and Fine Art

PO Box 357231, Gainesville, FL 32635-7231
Website: www.rafa.com
*Extensive collection of art, ceramics and pottery, art glass,
and items of the Arts and Crafts era*

Sattler's Stained Glass Studio, Ltd.

RR1, Pleasantville, NS, Canada B0R 1G0
Telephone: 902-688-1156 Fax: 902-688-1475
Repair, restoration, conservation, custom stained glass pieces

Sonoma Tilemakers

7750 Bell Road, Windsor, CA 95492
Telephone: 707-837-8177
Website: www.sonomatilemakers.com
*(sold through dealers). Makers of custom metal, art,
and glass tiles for use throughout the house*

Stone Origins

301 Pleasant Dr., Dallas, TX 75217
Telephone: 888-398-1299 Fax: 214-398-1293
Website: www.stoneorigins.com
E-mail: sales@stoneorigins.com
*Stone sinks; tile for countertops, backsplashes, floors, and
other uses*

Stone Source

215 Park Ave. S, New York, NY 10003
Telephone: 212-979-6400
Offices also in Boston, Chicago, Philadelphia, DC
Website: www.stonesource.com
E-mail: info@stonesource.com
*Burlington stone, limestone, marble, slate, granite;
plus ceramic, mosaic, and Veneto glass tiles*

Tile Restoration Center, Inc.

3511 Interlake N, Seattle, WA 98103
Telephone: 206-633-4866 Fax: 206-633-3489
Website: www.tilerestorationcenter.com
*Historically accurate Batchelder reproductions and Claycraft
designs*

Timeless Classic Elegance

3035 Barat Road, Montreal, Quebec,
Canada, H3Y 2H6
Telephone: 514-935-5196
Website: www.trocadero.com
E-mail: eserafini@timelessclassicelegance.com
Antique leaded stained glass windows from the UK

Trikeenan Tileworks

5 Main St., Keene, NH 03431
Telephone: 603-355-2961
Website: www.trikeenan.com
E-mail: showroomtrikeenan.com
Unique, hand-made tile, eclectic designs

C20 Twentieth Century Fires

2nd floor, Blankley House, Blankley St., Levenshulme,
Manchester M19 3PP UK
Telephone: +44 0161 225 1988
Fax: +44 0161 225 6466
Website: www.c20fires.co.uk
E-mail: sales@c20fires.co.uk
*Original and reproduction fireplaces, inserts, stoves, sur-
rounds, and tiles*

Urban Archaeology

143 Franklin St., New York, NY 10013
Telephone: 212-431-4646
*Custom historically accurate console sinks, washstands,
medicine cabinets, vanities; plus tile, mosaic, and stone*

Van Briggle Pottery

PO Box 96, Colorado Springs, CO 80901
Telephone: 800-847-6341
Website: www.vanbriggle.com
E-mail: info@vanbriggle.com
*The pottery founded by Artus Van Briggle in 1899 still pro-
duces many of its original Arts and Crafts and Art Nouveau
designs, including figurines, vases, and candleholders*

Walker Zanger

7055 Old Katy Rd., Houston, TX 77024
Telephone: 713-300-2940
Website: www.walkerzanger.com
*Showrooms in CA, NY, TX, FL, NV, GA, NC
Importer and distributor of a wide variety of stone and tile
for every application, from honed marble tiles to stone floor
medallions and hand-glazed ceramic tile, in classic and
unusual shapes*

WALLPAPER, TEXTILES, RUGS

Adelphi Paper Hangings
PO Box 494, The Plains, VA 20198
Telephone: 540-253-5367 Fax: 540-253-5388
Website: www.adelphipaperhangings.com
E-mail: anulet@aol.com
*Hand-joined, woodblock-printed wallpapers and borders, cus-
tom reproductions*

Ann Wallace & Friends

PO Box 2344, Venice, CA 90294
Telephone: 213-617-3310
Website: www.annwallace.com
E-mail: wallygab@earthlink.net
*Custom curtains in natural fibers, pillows, table runners,
fabric, patterns, embroidery kits, and curtain hardware*

Archive Edition Textiles

5427 Telegraph Ave., Oakland, CA 94609
Telephone: 510-654-1645 Fax: 510-654-1256
Website: www.textilestudio.com
E-mail: ACPtextile@aol.com
*Fine woven fabrics and finished textile products in authentic
period designs and colors*

Arts & Crafts Period Textiles

5427 Telegraph Ave., Oakland, CA 94609
Telephone: 510-654-1645
*Hand-embroidered, appliquéd, and stenciled curtains;
fabric, embroidery kits, and curtain hardware*

Asia Minor Carpets

236 Fifth Ave., 2nd Floor, New York, NY 10001
Telephone: 212-447-9066 Fax: 212-447-1879
Website: www.asiaminorcarpets.com
*Fine antique and newer Turkish carpets and kilims in
traditional and Arts and Crafts designs*

Bradbury & Bradbury Art Wallpapers

PO Box 155, Benicia, CA 94510
Telephone: 707-746-1900
Website: www.bradbury.com
*Extensive collection of hand silk-screened wallpaper in
period styles; full roomsets available for many styles*

Brewster Wallcovering

67 Pacella Park Dr., Randolph, MA 02368
Telephone: 800-366-1700, 781-963-4800
Website: www.brewsterwallcovering.com
E-mail: contactus@brewp.com
Traditional wallcovering, fabrics, and accessories

Burt Wall Papers

940 Tyler St., Unit #3, Benicia, CA 94510
Telephone: 707-745-4207
Website: www.burtwallpapers.com
Hand screen-printed reproduction wallpaper, custom work

Carol Mead Designs

949 Grant St., Benicia, CA 94510
Telephone: 707-747-0223
Website: www.carolmead.com
Wallpapers, prints, pillows, stationery

Carter & Co./Mt. Diablo Handprints

451 Ryder St., Vallejo, CA 94500
Telephone: 707-554-2682
Website: www.carterandco.com
E-mail: samples@carterandco.com
Extensive collection of hand-printed reproduction wallpaper

Charles Rupert Designs

2005 Oak Bay Ave., Victoria, BC V8R 1E5, Canada
Telephone: 250-592-4916
Website: www.charles-rupert.com

Reproduction wallpaper, fabrics, art tile, and home accessories in a number of styles

Craftsman Homes Connection

2525 E 29th, Suite 10B-343, Spokane, WA 99223
Telephone: 509-535-5098
Website: www.crafthome.com

Hand-chosen selection of furnishings for the Arts and Crafts home: rugs, pillows, needlework, lighting, stencils, vases, hardware, much more

Fair Oak Workshops

PO Box 5578, River Forest, IL 60305
Telephone: 800-341-0597 Fax: 708-366-3876
Website: www.fairoak.com

(Artisan collective) Reproduction lighting, metalware, pottery, textiles, stencils, jewelry and accessories

Farrow & Ball

1054 Yonge St., Toronto, ON
Telephone: 416-920-0200, 877-363-1040
E-mail: farrowball@bellnet.ca
Telephone: 845-369-4912 Fax: 845-369-4913
Website: www.farrow-ball.com
E-mail: usasales@farrow-ball.com

Manufacturers of traditional wallpapers and paints

Floor Couture

442 Rte. 202-206 N, Ste. 417, Bedminster, NJ 07921
Telephone: 908-575-8282 Fax: 908-575-8383
Website: www.floorcouture.com

Reproduction printed floorcloths and handpainted custom floorcloths

Historic Lighting

114 E Lemon Ave., Monrovia, CA 91016
Telephone: 626-303-4899
Website: www.HistoricLighting.com

Mission furniture, art pottery, hand-crafted carpets, period lighting and accessories; custom work

Inglenook Textiles

240 N Grand Ave., Pasadena, CA 91103
Telephone: 626-792-9729
Website: www.typeandstitch.com/inglenook.html
E-mail: itextiles@earthlink.net

Pillow and table runner kits in authentic designs, custom needlework available

J. R. Burrows & Company

PO Box 522, Rockland, MA 02370
Telephone: 800-347-1795, 781-982-1812
Fax: 781-982-1636
Website: www.burrows.com
E-mail: merchant@burrows.com

Arts and Crafts wallpaper, fabric, carpet, and lace curtains

Maine Wool + Design

145 Lisbon St., Ste. 701, Lewiston, ME 04240
Telephone: 207-784-9535 Fax: 207-784-7528
Website: www.rugdesign.com
E-mail: rugdesign@adelphia.net

Roycroft Collection: hand-tufted designer rugs in 100% New Zealand wool, silk-wool blends, and other specialty yarns

Mark Golding

25A Clifton Terrace, Brighton, Sussex BN1 3HA
Telephone: +44 0 1273 327774 / +44 0 7775 535453
Website: www.achome.co.uk
E-mail: mark@achome.co.uk

Morris wallpapers and fabrics, items by Voysey, Dresser, Godwin, Pugin, de Morgan, more

MKR Design

1504 E North Ave., Milwaukee, WI 53202
Telephone: 414-273-0463
Website: www.westernfurnishings.com
E-mail: info@westernfurnishings.com

Hand-tufted rugs in motifs suitable for Arts & Crafts and rustic interiors

Morris by Sanderson / Sanderson US

North America – showrooms in Boston, Atlanta, Toronto, Quebec, Alberta, and British Columbia
Website: www.sanderson-online.co.uk

Period-inspired fabrics, wallcoverings, bed linens, ready-made curtains and paint. The fabrics and wallcoverings in the Morris & Co. collection are from original William Morris documents.

Nature's Loom

29 E 32nd St., New York, NY 10016
Telephone: 800-365-2002 Fax: 212-213-8414
Website: www.naturesloom.com
E-mail: info@naturesloom.com

Hand-made rugs in Arts & Crafts-inspired designs

New River Artisans

Showrooms in Atlanta, Denver, Indianapolis, Salt Lake City, and High Point, NC
PO Box 1, 528 Piney Creek School Rd., Piney Creek, NC 28663
Telephone: 336-359-2216 Fax: 336-359-2234
Website: www.newriverartisans.com

USA-made fine custom wool rugs in any size, shape, color or design; standard Arts and Crafts designs available.

Noonoo Rug Co.

100 Park Plaza Dr. #209, Secaucus, NJ 07094
Telephone: 201-330-0101
Website: www.noonoorug.com

Hand-made Oriental carpets in Arts & Crafts, traditional, and modern styles

Old Ways Ltd.

39 Barton Ave. SE, Minneapolis, MN 55414
Telephone: 612-379-2142
Website: www.oldwaysltd.com

Hand-crafted tabletop furniture, housewares, textiles, endpapers

Persian Carpet Company

5634 Chapel Hill Blvd., Durham, NC 27707
Telephone: 800-333-1801, 919-489-8362
Website: www.persiancarpet.com

Antique and new hand-loomed carpets in British and American Arts and Crafts styles

Pendleton Woodworks

2631 Island Hwy. W, Qualicum Beach, BC V9K 1G7, CA
Telephone: 250-752-1184
Website: www.pendletonwoodworks.com

Arts and Crafts-style stained glass lamps, furniture, accessories, fabrics

Sanderson US / Morris by Sanderson

North America – showrooms in Boston, Atlanta, Toronto, Quebec, Alberta, and British Columbia
Website: www.sanderson-online.co.uk

Period-inspired fabrics, wallcoverings, bed linens, ready-made curtains and paint. The fabrics and wallcoverings in the Morris & Co. collection are from original William Morris documents.

Scalamandré

942 Third Ave., New York, NY 10022
Telephone: 800-932-4361
Website: www.scalamandre.com

Traditional and reproduction historical textiles, trimmings, wallpaper, and carpet

Thibaut

480 Frelinghuysen Ave., Newark, NJ 07114
Telephone: 800-223-0704, 973-643-1118
Fax: 973-643-3133
Website: www.thibautdesign.com
E-mail: info@thibautdesign.com

Wallpapers and fabrics since 1886, historic collection of wallpapers duplicates antique printing methods

Thistle Handwerks

PO Box 21578, Billings, MT 59104
Telephone: 406-896-9434
Website: www.thistlehandwerks.com
E-mail: thistlehandwerks@earthlink.net

Custom linen work in the Glasgow School of Embroidery and Clarence Crafters styles

Thistle Hill Weavers

101 Chestnut Ridge Rd., Cherry Valley, NY 13320
Telephone: 518-284-2729, 866-384-2729
Website: www.thistlehillweavers.com

Replicated fabrics from the 17th, 18th, and 19th centuries

Trustworth Studios
P.O. Box 1109, Plymouth, MA 02362
Telephone: 508-746-1847 Fax: 508-746-3736
Website: www.trustworth.com
E-mail: voyseyboy@trustworth.com
Custom period lighting, wallpaper, clocks, furniture; needlework and accessories in the Voysey lin

Tufenkian Carpets
902 Broadway, Second Floor,
New York, NY 10010-6002
Telephone: 800-475-4788
Website: www.tufenkiancarpets.com
Hand-crafted carpets in Persian and Arts and Crafts styles

United Crafts
127 W Putnam Ave., #123, Greenwich, CT 06830
Telephone: 203-869-4898
Website: www.unitedcrafts.com
E-mail: merchant@unitedcrafts.com
Hand-made small textiles, reproduction bronze candlesticks, hand-glazed stoneware, wool rugs and dhurries

Victorian Collectibles Ltd.
845 E Glenbrook Rd., Milwaukee, WI 53217
Telephone: 800-783-3829
Website: www.victorianwallpaper.com
E-mail: vcl@victorianwallpaper.com
Authentic restoration wallpapers, borders, ceiling papers and treatments

Waterhouse Wallhangings
260 Maple St., Chelsea, MA 02150
Telephone: 617-884-8222
Reproduction 19th century American and English wallpapers (sales to the trade only)

Wolff House Art Papers LLC
133 S Main St., Mt. Vernon, OH 43050
Telephone: 740-397-9466 Fax: 740-397-9467
Website: www.wolffhousewallpapers.com
E-mail: studio@wolffhousewallpapers.com
Extensive collection of hand-screened historic wallpaper in period styles; custom reproduction work available

Wright Style
10580 Newkirk St., Suite 302, Dallas, TX 75220-2329
Telephone: 877-858-0913
Fax: 972-409-0082
Website: www.wrightstyle.com
Framed art, textile art, dinnerware, ornaments, trivets, doormats and others based on designs of Frank Lloyd Wright

OTHER

C. J. Hurley Century Arts
3247 NE Glisan St., Portland, OR 97232
Telephone: 503-234-4167
Website: www. cjhurley.com
Custom interiors, period-style artwork, gesso panels, and consultation

Charleston Gardens
650 King St., Charleston, SC 29403
Telephone: 800-469-0118
Website: www.charlestongardens.com
Everything imaginable for outdoor living, from arbors and gazebos to garden and cottage-style furniture and freestanding statuary

Cherry Tree Design
320 Pronghorn Trail, Bozeman, MT 59718
Telephone: 800-634-3268 Fax: 406-582-8444
Website: www.cherrytreedesign.com
Lighting, screens, mirrors, and accessories made in the Arts and Crafts tradition

Dard Hunter Studios
Mountain House, 8 Highland Ave., PO Box 771,
Chillicothe, OH 45601
Telephone: 740-774-1236 Fax: 740-779-3273
Website: www.dardhunter.com
E-mail: info@dardhunter.com
(Roycroft) Pottery, frames, paper and prints, jewelry, more; maintained by the grandson of Dard Hunter

Epoch Designs
PO Box 4033, Elwyn, PA 19063
Telephone: 610-565-9180
Website: www.epochdesigns.com
E-mail: info@epochdesigns.com
Authentic period-style stencils

Fair Oak Workshops
PO Box 5578, River Forest, IL 60305
Telephone: 800-341-0597 Fax: 708-366-3876
Website: www.fairoak.com
(artisan collective) Reproduction lighting, metalware, pottery, textiles, stencils, jewelry and accessories

Fine Lines Framemakers
PO Box 412, Belvidere, NJ 07823
Telephone: 800-294-7973 Fax: 610-588-8185
Website: www.finelinesframing.com
E-mail: info@finelinesframing.com
Individually designed, hand crafted Craftsman-style frames and mirrors in hardwoods

Haddonstone
201 Heller Pl., Bellmawr, NJ 08031
Telephone: 856-931-7011
Website: www. haddonstone.com
Classic landscape ornaments and architectural stonework

Helen Foster Stencils
PO Box 5578, River Forest, IL 60305
Telephone: 800-341-0597 Fax: 708-366-3876
Website: www.fairoak.com
E-mail: sales@fairoak.com
Arts and Crafts stencils in authentic and period-inspired styles

Hill House Antiques & Decorative Arts
PO Box 17320, 18 Chelsea Manor Street,
London SW3 2WR UK
Telephone: +44 0 7973 842777
Website: www.hillhouse-antiques.co.uk
Metalware, ceramics, small furniture, pictures and prints, more

Holton Studios Frame Makers
5515 Doyle St. #2, Emeryville, CA 94608
Telephone: 510-450-0350
Website: www.holtonframes.com
Specializing in Arts and Crafts frames and mirrors, broad selection and custom designs

Hyde Park Fine Art of Moldings, Inc.
29-16 40th Ave., Long Island City, NY 11101
Telephone: 718-706-0504 Fax: 718-706-0507
Website: www.hyde-park.com
E-mail: info@hyde-park.com
Hand-crafted plaster moldings and trim in period styles

John Canning Painting & Conservation Studios
125 Commerce Ct. #5, Cheshire, CT 06410
Telephone: 203-272-9868 Fax: 203-272-9879
Website: www.canning-studios.com
E-mail: info@canning-studios.com
Conservation and restoration of a wide range of finishes, fine art and decorative elements, new design

Kathleen West Printmaker
PO Box 545, 159 Maple St., East Aurora, NY 14052
Telephone: 716-652-9125
Website: www.kathleenwest.com
E-mail: kathleenwest@kathleenwest.com
(Roycroft Master Artisan) Limited edition, hand-colored Arts and Crafts block prints in the Roycroft tradition

Milestone Ltd.
4225 NE 9th Ave., Amarillo, TX 79107
Telephone: 888-851-3381, 806-381-4030
Fax: 806-381-6996
Website: www.milestoneltd.com
Hand-cast architectural concrete ornamental stone and decorative elements, custom work

Mitchell Andrus Studios
68 Central Ave., Stirling, NJ 07980
Telephone: 908-647-7442 Fax: 908-647-4090
Website: www.mitchellandrus.com
(Roycroft Renaissance Artisan) Furniture and accessories in authentic arts and Crafts styles, custom framing also

Old Ways Ltd.
39 Barton Ave. SE, Minneapolis, MN 55414
Telephone: 612-379-2142
Website: www.oldwaysltd.com
Hand-crafted tabletop furniture, housewares, textiles, endpapers

Pratt & Lambert

PO Box 22, Buffalo, NY 14240
Telephone: 800-289-7728
Website: www.prattandlambert.com

Color Guide for Historical Homes, depicting tints for different eras including Arts and Crafts; dealers nationwide

Randall Antiques and Fine Art

PO Box 357231, Gainesville, FL 32635-7231
Website: www.rafa.com

Extensive collection of art, ceramics and pottery, art glass, and items of the Arts and Crafts era

Reggio Register

PO Box 511, 20 Central Ave., Ayer, MA 01432
Telephone: 800-880-3090
Website: www.reggioregister.com

Manufactures a complete line of hand-crafted, cast-iron, cast-brass, cast-aluminum, and solid wood registers and grilles

Sherwin Williams

101 Prospect Ave., Cleveland, OH 44115
Telephone: 216-566-2000
Website: www.Sherwin-williams.com

(sold through local dealers) Interior and exterior paints: their Preservation Palette includes Arts and Crafts colors

The Swan Company

5956 County Rd. 200, Orland, CA 95963
Telephone: 530-865-4109
Website: www.swanpicturehangers.com

Picture hanging paraphernalia, including tassels, moulding, hooks, nails, picture rails, cord, and chain

Tinay Wicker

11426 40th Ave E, Tacoma, WA 98446
Telephone: 253-468-2498
Website: www.tinaystudio.com
E-mail: peeta@tinaystudio.com

Hand-crafted wicker planters, baskets and accessories patterned after early 20th century originals

Trellis Structures

PO Box 380, 60 River St., Rear, Beverly, MA 01915
Telephone: 888-285-4624, 978-921-1235
Fax: 978-232-1151
Website: www.trellisstructures.com
E-mail: sales@trellisstructures.com

High quality garden structures in classic and unique designs, constructed of clear western red cedar and mahogany: arbors, trellises, garden arches, pergolas, garden furniture and accents

Trimbelle River Studio & Design

PO Box 568, Ellsworth, WI 54011
Telephone: 715-273-4844 Fax: 715-273-4806
Website: www.trimbelleriver.com
E-mail: info@trimbelleriver.com

Period reproduction stencils and supplies

United Crafts

127 W Putnam Ave., #123, Greenwich, CT 06830
Telephone: 203-869-4898
Website: www.unitedcrafts.com
E-mail: merchant@unitedcrafts.com

Hand-made small textiles, reproduction bronze candlesticks, hand-glazed stoneware, wool rugs and dhurries

Vermont Soapstone

PO Box 268, 248 Stoughton Pond Rd., Perkinsville, VT 05151-0268
Telephone: 802-263-5404 Fax: 802-263-9451
Website: www.vermontsoapstone.com
E-mail: sales@vermontsoapstone.com

Custom manufacturers of architectural soapstone products for throughout the home